# Everything I Know

*Basic Life Rules
from a
Jewish Mother*

# Sharon Strassfeld

SCRIBNER

SCRIBNER
1230 Avenue of the Americas
New York, NY 10020

SCRIBNER and design are trademarks of
Simon & Schuster Inc.

Designed by Brooke Zimmer
Set in Fournier Monotype
Manufactured in the United States of America

1   3   5   7   9   10   8   6   4   2

Library of Congress Cataloging-in-Publication Data
Strassfeld, Sharon.
Everything I know: basic life rules from a Jewish mother/
Sharon Strassfeld.
p.   cm.
1. Jewish way of life.   2. Strassfeld, Sharon—Family.
3. Jews—United States—Anecdotes.   I. Title.
BM723.S73   1998
296.7—dc21      98-17763
CIP
ISBN 0-684-84725-6

*For Kayla, Noam, and Ben,*
*the ones I love best*

# Acknowledgments

I OFTEN READ THE acknowledgments in books and find them too long and too sweetly false. So you can rest assured this will be mercifully brief and absolutely true. I've never worked with an agent before, so I had no expectations about what such an addition in my life might mean. Nancy Trichter, as it turns out, is someone who believes in a project, is helpful with suggestions, is willing to spend time talking through ideas, is respectful about the writing process, and always does what she says she is going to do. More than this one cannot, in good conscience, ask of anyone, and I would work with Nancy again in a New York minute. Jane Rosenman is a wonderful editor, always respectful about language, gently provocative in the issues she raises, and able to prod me to delve deeper than I think I can. I like people who push me and I have a lot of respect for Jane.

Thanks to my buddies who read early drafts of the manuscript and helped critique it: Bill Novak (who also spent an hour thinking up titles with me), Merle Feld, Everett and Mary Gendler, Ann Appelbaum and Neal Borovitz, Judy Peck, Sonny, and Mark and Debby. You guys are the best!

# Introduction

THIS BOOK CAME ABOUT because my mother never had any jewelry except for her engagement ring. I envied, with a fierce ache, my friends who, when choosing a pin or necklace to wear, would say to me, "I can see my mother right now wearing this pin." I understood this to be one of the many mother-bonds that would forever elude me. For my own daughter Kayla's Bat Mitzvah gift, I determined to buy her a piece of fine jewelry. I called Cousin Lewis, the jeweler, and explained my quest. He replied that he had just the thing for me, since he had recently acquired a matched pair of 24-karat-gold Art Deco bracelets that singly could be worn by a teenager but paired would be dramatic and beautiful for an adult. I was thrilled and bought them immediately, imagining myself giving Kayla one bracelet for her Bat Mitzvah and the other four years later when she graduated from high school.

I gave Kayla the first bracelet the day before her Bat Mitzvah and she, generous soul that she is, thanked me and told me how lovely the bracelet was. Kayla never wore it—not then, nor in the years following (nor, so far as I know, to this day). I had leisure in the ensuing years to mull over the undeniable fact that my longings for my own mother had trapped me. For her Bat Mitzvah, I had not looked fully into my daughter's face to read her heart, and I made a vow in my own heart to do better when she graduated from high school.

Four years later, as the date for Kayla's departure to college drew closer, I was overwhelmed by the sadness of our incipient parting. For those of us who have done it, letting our first child leave home, knowing that in all likelihood he will never return, that her leaving spells the end to the warm, connected, safe family we have spent years trying to build, is an agonizing process. About six months before Kayla left for college, I began to think about my home-leaving gift to her. I found myself yearning to give her armor/treasure to take on her journey—something that in her eyes would have value not only for that moment but forever in her life.

I asked myself, "What will Kayla need to make her own way in life?" "Nothing I have to give her anymore," I answered sadly. But the conviction began to grow in me that I hadn't taught her enough about my own life-truths. I hadn't conveyed the hard-won wisdom I had learned/earned for myself, nor had I told her enough family stories in a concentrated, rather than desultory, fashion for her roots to be, in my mind, satisfactorily entwined with those of her ancestors. I began to jot down notes over the next four months—all the things I needed her to know before I could let her go with a peaceful mind (mine, not hers). I gave Kayla a twenty-page book just before she graduated high school, and I know in the ensuing years she has taken it with her whenever she has moved or traveled.

WHEN IT came time for my second child, Noam, to leave home, I reread what I had written to Kayla and realized two things: my relationship with Noam was different from my relationship with Kayla, and he himself was a very different person. Therefore, the things I wanted to tell him were different. I gave him his own book (along with a copy of Kayla's so I wouldn't have to repeat) and he, being who he is, can't find it. (Incidentally, I have one more child still to go. Ben is only ten years old as I write this, and I'll have to hope that I learn new things in the next eight years so he won't feel cheated out of a book when his time comes.) This, then, is my graduation present to each of my children.

Dear Kayla:

I've spent the last eighteen years of my life (roughly paralleling the same eighteen years of your life) thinking about you. I vowed when I had children I would pay attention to them and spend time understanding in a deep way who they are. I vowed I would accept every part of my children—even the parts that were foreign to me.

Instead, with all the best intentions in the world, I found myself sometimes bewildered by you, puzzled by your very being. You were so deeply reticent as a child (less so now), so sensitive emotionally, so acute intellectually, and so cautious instinctually (I well remember trying to coax, cajole, bribe, and bully you into trying the alpine slide at Jiminy Peak!) that I marveled at God's mixing of the genetic patterns.

You know (I think) that I adore you. I will deeply miss your presence in my daily life. Besides adoring you, I enjoy your company. You are so many things that I could never be that I also admire you tremendously. All my life I have longed for the grace, tranquillity, and serenity that are so naturally a part of who you are. Your unfailing support to those you love, your unflappability, your ability to see acutely yet never to judge harshly, are all traits I value in you. You have always been a source of joy and pride to me and I pray that whoever you find to love in your life will be a person worthy of a gift like you.

I know you are uncomfortable with this letter and I apologize for making you feel that way. What I want to do is give you this book as your leaving-home present. In it, I will tell you the family stories I want you to remember and will teach you all the life-truths that I have access to. There are, of course, other life-truths you'll need to know in your life, but those life-truths I don't know, so you'll have to acquire them on your own or from others. Some of what I have to tell you is going to seem pretty trivial, I'm sure. Perhaps the lesson is that trivial things also have their own importance. So, here goes—and in no particular order . . .

Love,

eema

Dear Noam:

My grandmother used to say that if God didn't cause us to forget the pain of the birth an hour later, the universe would cease to exist. In your case, I have never forgotten the exquisite pain of your birth—so very different from Kayla's far more gentle entry—nor have I ever forgotten how awestruck I felt by the force of the power and vitality with which you burst into this world. Such was your beginning, such is your nature.

In the seventeen years since your birth, I have continued to be dazzled by your wild exuberance, your infectious laughter, your impish charm, your knowing insouciance, the vividness and vitality of your colors. Kathy Green often reminds me that I used to watch you when you were one year old climbing fearlessly up to the highest monkey bars in the playground and I would say, "This child is in my *kishkes*." Kathy knew what I meant—that you were, in the essence of your being, deeply familiar to me. I felt then, and continue to feel today, that I know who you are because who you are is so genetically linked to who I am. I can feel my own blood, bones, sinew, muscle, and soul buried deep in your body. You have never been "other" to me. (I can also feel my friend Leah, the psychiatrist, at this very moment sighing sadly over what I've just written.)

The very exuberance you bring to your life often makes

you impatient. I well remember the summer you were eleven years old when, after unpacking your trunk when you came home from camp, I found more than a dozen of my letters to you that you had never even opened! That trait persists in you to this day, and as I write this, some part of me does indeed wonder if you will have the patience to read this book through to the end. I console myself with the thought that I am writing this as a long-term gift to you. What you don't read on the first sitting may be something you read five years from now. Or, knowing you, perhaps not.

Now the hard part. I know that at times I have failed you. I've been impatient with your disorganization, with the chaos that reigns around you (I shudder to this day when I remember the state of the kitchen after you began your experiments in learning to bake popovers), with the fact that (I know you think this is a secret) when you don't feel like putting your clean laundry away, you throw it back into the hamper, with your leaving your things all over the house, with your borrowing things and then losing them. You never seem fazed by my evident disapproval or disgruntlement, and sometimes I find myself laughing over the chaos you create for yourself. (I understand how, coming home from Oren's house, you could get on the train the wrong way and end up on Long Island instead of in Manhattan— but how could you do it *twice*?!). But truth to tell, you have not been easy to live with. And truth to tell, I am going to miss your living here every day of my life.

Your gifts to me have been manifold. You are the one in the family who notices me and notices and cares most about what is going on in my life. You have a deep and sensitive instinct about people—although only your most intimate friends know this about you, partly because you use your infectious joie de vivre as a bit of a shield. In truth, you are one of the most intuitive people I've ever met—you have the astonishing ability to cut to the heart of the matter and see clearly what is going on in a situation. You were the one who said to me once when I was complaining about how exhausted I was after work and how I'd like to retire and never have to work again, "Eema, you *love* your work. You wouldn't give it up for anything!" You, with your seven-year-old intuition, knew that truth and cut to the heart with one observation. I *love* that quality in you. After all the Sturm und Drang over any given subject, I can always count on you to come through with a dry observation that will at once illuminate and clarify for all of us.

I also love the part of you that nurtures. You like to be helpful to other people; you care about those you love and you are not at all afraid to show it. I believe that these gifts will warm you and those around you all your life. I well remember the generosity of spirit that impelled you to speak to a twelve-year-old boy you barely knew one Yom

Kippur because you noticed, as the day wore on, how difficult he seemed to find fasting for the first time. I overheard you reassuring him that it had been hard for you too the first time you fasted, but that he could get through it. And he did—in no small part because you had noticed his panic and taken the time to address it. That is a *very* rare quality.

You never actually read the book I wrote to Kayla when she graduated from high school, so you're probably wondering what this is all about. This, dear son, is my graduation present to you. It's a book of my life-truths and our family stories and information. I'll give you, with this, a copy of Kayla's book so that I won't have to repeat anything. I know, knowing you, that you are really wishing for a new computer for your graduation present. I'm sure you will look with quickly concealed dismay at this book when I give it to you and think wildly to yourself, "This is *it*?" I work like a dog to graduate high school, and she gives me this *book of family wisdom as a reward*?! This is some cruel joke!" The knowledge that that is what you will secretly be thinking will make me chuckle my way through this writing. So here, dear son, is your graduation present, with all my love . . .

eema

דַּע מֵאַיִן בָּאתָ, וּלְאָן אַתָּה הוֹלֵךְ,
וְלִפְנֵי מִי אַתָּה עָתִיד לִתֵּן דִּין וְחֶשְׁבּוֹן.

*Know where you come from,*
*Where you are going,*
*And before whom you will one day stand in judgement . . .*
Ethics of the Fathers 3:1

# Everything I Know

# Know where you come from . . .

My mother told me this story once when I was young. I asked her how she could tell that her mother loved her. The reason I asked my mother this is that my *bubbee* (grandmother), Chai-Raizel, was a very strong woman. She could be very dictatorial, critical, and even abusive to her children (although she was never that way to me—I adored her). Because of Chai-Raizel's constant criticisms, I could never understand how my mother was sure she was loved. She told me that she found out her mother loved her once when she was a little girl, and she never forgot it. What happened was this. Upstairs from where my mother lived as a girl lived a woman named Mrs. Hominoff. Mrs. Hominoff had an only son. One day, when a hurricane was predicted and the foul weather had already begun, Mrs. Hominoff called my mother upstairs and asked her to go to the store. My mother went to the store and delivered the groceries to Mrs. Hominoff. When my mother returned home, Chai-Raizel asked her where she had been. She explained that Mrs. Hominoff had sent her to the store for groceries. My grandmother marched upstairs and demanded to know why Mrs. Hominoff had sent her daughter Ruchel to the store in the rain. My mother listened in the stairwell and heard Mrs. Hominoff explain to my grandmother that since my grandmother had four daughters, all, thank God, healthy, and since she herself had only one son, she had asked Ruchel to go. At this, my grandmother drew in her breath sharply and answered with a fierce anger: "Mrs. Hominoff, I don't have four daughters. I have only one daughter. I have one Libbe, one Ruchel, one Miriamele, and one Yette. So the next time you need something from the store, never again send my one daughter!"

In our family, to this day, we never walk around the house in socks without shoes. We consider this to be a sign of mourning (because a mourner is not allowed to wear leather and so could often be found during shiva in socks without shoes). When I would slip up occasionally as a child, my *bubbee*, Chai-Raizel, who was never stern with me, would reprimand me firmly.

My mother used to endure our good-natured teasing about her constantly taking pictures whenever the family was together. Now I am incredibly grateful to her for those faded, blurry pictures because they serve as a visual documentary of our life together. So . . . everywhere you go, *take pictures.* You will never regret it.

My mother was adamant that we never sew anything while the person was wearing the garment (i.e., that we not sew a button on while the coat was being worn). Someone years later told me that the superstition arose because the only time a person remains passive while something is being done to him is when the person is dead and his body is being prepared for purification, dressing, and burial. Therefore, the custom in some families was not to do anything like sewing a garment while the wearer stood passively waiting. If it is absolutely necessary to sew a garment while it is being worn, the person who is wearing the garment must chew on a cracker or on something else the whole time.

My mother loved sweet corn so much that she would eat it until she made herself sick. I loved this quality in my mother.

There is a story connected to the diamond ring I wear. My mother, who was from the poorer side of the family, got engaged to my father at the same time that her wealthy cousin Adele got engaged to Lenny. Lenny gave Adele a beautiful diamond engagement ring. My father had saved up much of his army pay and was about to choose a ring for my mother when she forestalled him. "Uncle Abe, the head of the family, asked me to bring you to Elizabeth, New Jersey, so he could meet you. He also said he would talk to you then about a ring." The next weekend my mother and father made the trip from Providence to Elizabeth and Uncle Abe met my father. He sent my mother from the room and asked whether my father had bought the engagement ring for his niece yet. "Not yet," replied my father. "I was going to do it next week." Uncle Abe then asked, "How much money have you set aside to buy it?" "I've saved up two hundred and fifty dollars!" replied my father proudly. "Don't buy anything," said Uncle Abe. "I have a connection in the jewelry business and can get it for you wholesale. You come back next weekend and I will have the ring for you then." The next weekend my father brought Uncle Abe the $250 and in return Uncle Abe gave him a 2 1/2-carat diamond ring in a platinum setting surrounded by baguettes. My father, who remains as naive and trusting some fifty years later as he was that day, thanked Uncle Abe, returned to Providence, and brought the ring to his sister to show it to her before giving it to my mother. Aunt Shirley gasped when she saw the ring and asked in amazement, "Where did you ever get the money for that ring?" "Ruthie's uncle has a connection in the diamond business. The ring cost two hundred and fifty dollars," he explained to her. "Two hundred and fifty dollars!" she replied in astonishment as she reached into her drawer. "Here is two hundred and fifty dollars. I want a ring just like Ruthie's." My father took the money and went back to New Jersey later that week. He handed Uncle Abe the money and said, "My sister wants a ring just like the one you got for

Ruthie." Uncle Abe handed him back the money and explained gravely, but with a certain twinkle, "Such a ring, Saul, happens only once in a lifetime."

About the same ring there is another story. I never knew my mother had an engagement ring because she never wore it. I think perhaps my mother thought wearing expensive jewelry was ostentatious, but I am not sure. Whatever the reason, when Kayla was nine months old, my mother called from Providence at six in the morning one day and said, "I'm getting on the seven A.M. train and coming into New York for a visit. I'll be there by eleven." At 11:15 A.M. the doorbell rang and my mother came in and handed me a crumpled tissue. "Here," she said. "This is for Kayla. Put it away for her until she's old enough to have it." I unwrapped the tissue and stared in astonishment at the ring I never knew my mother had owned. I was overwhelmed by hurt that she had not decided to pass her one piece of jewelry on to me, her only daughter. I, of course, understood that while my mother's relationship with me was complicated—entwined and occasionally even gnarled—my mother's relationship with my daughter was unrestrained, loving, and gentle, but knowing this did not lessen my sense of rejection. Wordlessly, I handed it back to her and, unable to summon the words to explain my hurt, only said stonily, "I will not be the caretaker of your gifts to my daughter. If you want her to have it, give it to her yourself when you think she is ready to have it." My mother, who knew me very well, understood, and was furious with me. She took the ring without a word, rewrapped it in the tissue, and left the house. Four hours later, at 4:00 P.M., the phone rang. "It's me," said my mother. "I'm back in Providence. But I'm getting back on the train and I'll be there in four hours." Sure enough, four hours later my doorbell rang for the second time that day. My mother walked into the house and handed me the tissue. "You were right," she said, looking me straight in the eye. "The ring is for you." "If you give it to me, then it's mine," I said. "I can do anything I want with it." "Yes," she replied, "you can." "I can even wear it," I announced blandly. My mother gulped audibly but said, "Yes, you can wear it. It's really yours." I put the ring away for a month and thought about it. Then, after a month, I took it out, put it on my finger, and I have never taken it off since.

My mother searched for "American" recipes to cook for my sweet sixteen party. She asked her coworkers for suggestions, and one Italian woman gave her this recipe for spinach loaf, which became a family favorite. Defrost a loaf of frozen bread dough (which in our family meant challah dough but, not surprisingly, in the original recipe meant Italian bread). In a separate bowl, defrost 4 to 5 packages of frozen chopped spinach. When it is fully defrosted, squeeze out all the water from the spinach. Then add 1 can of pitted black olives, chopped up, and 6 cloves of fresh garlic, chopped fine. Add lots of salt (preferably kosher salt), some black pepper, 3 beaten eggs, and a few tablespoons of olive oil. Smash the challah dough flat into a rectangular sheet. Put the spinach mix in a roll down the middle of the challah dough. Roll the challah up jelly-roll style and pinch shut. Put the roll seam side down on a greased cookie sheet. Bake uncovered at 350 degrees until brown.

My mother taught me to buy long, thin carrots because they are sweeter. Aunty Sarah did not believe this was so.

Many years ago, when I was dating your father, my mother said to me, "If you want to understand who you will be marrying, *kik auf der mama*" (literally, "look at the mother"). I responded, as I often did in those days, "Ma, don't give me a lot of that eastern European voodoo. I know who I'll be marrying because I spend time with him and because I know him." Now here it is twenty-seven years later and I know that my mother was right. If you truly want to understand who it is your partner will be one day, it's important to look at the person's parents. If you don't admire and respect them, be careful.

My mother was a woman who did many good deeds quietly, without anyone ever knowing about them. One of the things she did was to cook each week for a crippled man whose wife had left him. I did not know until shortly before she died that she had done this.

All her life my mother wanted to own a freezer. She never bought herself one, although she and my father had enough money to do so. When I moved to New York, I bought a freezer. My mother used to visit my freezer often. She would bake things and bring them as a gift for my freezer. She would check out my meat supply and add to it. She derived tremendous, if wistful, enjoyment from my freezer. And she died without ever having owned her own freezer. This has been a lesson to me all my life. If you really want something, it's not good to delay too long in getting it.

The other story in our family that corroborates the freezer story is this one. When I was graduating from high school, I desperately wanted to leave Rhode Island and go to Stern College. My parents were adamant that I attend the University of Rhode Island. We were at loggerheads until finally we all got into the car to travel to Elizabeth, New Jersey, to seek an *aitzah* (advice) from Uncle Abe. Uncle Abe sat us all down in his dining room. He listened to me speak about my deep and fervent desire to go to Stern. Then he sent me out of the room to talk to my parents. After a while he called me back into the room and told me I would be allowed to go to Stern. Sometime later I asked Uncle Abe why my parents had agreed. He replied, "In life, it is not good to want something as much as you wanted Stern and not, if it's possible, to have it."

Uncle Abe was an enormously stubborn man. In a family filled with stubborn people, he was known as the intractable one. He owned an umbrella factory in New York City. He treated his workers fairly and had a good relationship with many of them. One day, a representative from a local union stood outside his factory making the acquaintance of Uncle Abe's workers and a few weeks later succeeded in convincing the factory workers to unionize. The foreman came to Uncle Abe and told him that the workers planned to unionize the plant. Uncle Abe responded by warning him that he would not tolerate a union in his plant. The man said that nonetheless the matter was going to a vote and he fully expected that the decision to unionize would be ratified. Then Uncle Abe said, "I warn you. If my workers decide to join a union, I will shut down this plant. I will never allow a union to tell me how to run my business!" The man assumed that Uncle Abe was bluffing and the vote was scheduled and ratified the following week. Two days later, after the factory closed that night, Uncle Abe backed up a truck to the factory, loaded up all the manufacturing equipment, padlocked the door, and shut down his umbrella business.

Many families have stories about feuds that were so powerful, the warring family members didn't speak to each other for decades. I used to think this was ridiculous until it happened to me. Here's the story. You know that I was raised in an extended family. My brother, Mark, and I had three cousins, Marty, Stevie, and Harvey, who lived around one corner and two cousins, Susan and Robin, who lived around the other corner. We were in and out of each other's homes on an hourly basis. As children, we took trips together, ate together, played together, fought with each other, and, in general, had a kind of extended brother-sister relationship. As we grew older and changed (Marty and Stevie became quite religious), some of us were no longer in touch with the others. My oldest cousin Marty moved to Israel and got married there. I visited Israel shortly after his marriage and, although we had not been close in many years, I called to wish him *mazel tov*. He invited all of us to his new apartment for dinner. I enjoyed the evening and enjoyed meeting his new bride. The next week, I called to reciprocate and invite them for dinner at the apartment we were renting during our vacation. Marty explained that he would not come to our apartment for dinner, since he did not know how kosher our landlord was. I offered to have any kosher caterer or restaurant of his choice bring in food and new dishes. He refused. I offered to do anything he wanted to make it possible for him to eat in the home we were renting that summer. I told him that cost was no issue: whatever he wanted we would accommodate. Marty again refused and instead invited me back to his home. By now we were both very upset, Marty maintaining that the point was for all of us to spend time together, me maintaining that his rules were about power, not about religion. I ended the conversation by telling him the following: "For me, this is a very simple mathematical construct. My family eats in my home. You do not eat in my home. If you do not eat in my home, you are not my family. Period." We did not speak for ten years. I did not particularly miss the relationship, since we had long before grown apart. Several times in those years, Harvey, sweet soul that he is, tried to make peace. Each time he did, I explained to him that, contrary to what he and others believed in the family, I was not angry at Marty. I just felt strongly about being able to have my family over to dinner. Then, three years ago, Marty's mother, my aunt Libby, lay dying in a nursing home in Israel. I called the home quite frequently to see how she was doing. One of those times, Marty answered the phone and I asked after his mother. He told me that she was failing quickly and we shared our sadness. Three months after she died, I visited Israel and Marty called me. He said one of the things his mother had felt most strongly about was that there should be peace in the family. I replied that I knew this was true. My aunt had always been a true believer in keeping the family together; she herself had suffered many indignities in her life rather than create a breach in the family. Marty then said, "I would like to invite you to my home for dinner during your visit." I replied that although it was nice to have reestablished a connection with him, I could not go to his home for dinner without being able to reciprocate. For me, nothing really had changed. "Then," said Marty, "would you invite me to your home?" I was delighted and he came to dinner some days afterward. We talked, uneasily, about our individual understandings of the entire incident. Not surprisingly, our versions did not agree. But, with no small degree of awkwardness and pain, we are trying to learn again how to be in a family together.

There was another, earlier feud in our family. When I was seven years old, my mother's youngest sister, Yetty, got engaged. Yetty asked her cousin Lee, who bad recently gotten a divorce, to be her matron of honor at the wedding. My grandmother was at that time dying of cancer, and everyone knew that this was the last celebration she would live to attend. My mother, Ruth, thought it would be important to my grandmother if all four daughters—Libby, Ruth, Miriam, and Yetty—stood under the *huppah* together. She discussed it with her sister Yetty, who thought the idea was a good one but refused to ask Cousin Lee to withdraw as matron of honor so that Libby could serve. My mother took it upon herself to go to Lee's mother, Aunt Clara, to ask her to intervene with Lee. Aunt Clara, not surprisingly, refused. My mother was furious and refused to speak to Aunt Clara and Lee for many, many years. I don't know why my mother finally decided to reestablish relations with her aunt, but I do know they became very close in Aunt Clara's last years. I knew the story of the feud because, as a child, I listened surreptitiously to my mother discussing her feelings with her sisters, none of whom would have told her she was wrong even if they believed it in their hearts. As a child of seven, I puzzled over the feud, trying to understand why standing under a *huppah* would be so important to my mother or my grandmother. I kept feeling that there was some value at stake that I was simply too young to understand. When I was forty years old, more than a decade after my mother had died, I helped to organize a family reunion. One morning at the reunion, I was preparing breakfast in the kitchen with Lee's two sisters. "Do you remember when my mother stopped speaking to your side of the family?" I asked in the lull between all the reminiscences. "Sure," replied Adele. "She was so superstitious, she couldn't tolerate the thought of a divorced person standing under the *huppah* at her youngest sister's wedding." I remember the sunlight streaming through the window at that very moment as all the connections finally clicked into place in my mind. That had been the piece that was missing all along and it only took me thirty-three years to hear the rest of the story.

Kayla, you spoke to me recently about how, as a child, you were sometimes frightened by my anger. That anger is one of my mother's legacies to me. I've learned, over the course of many years of introspection, to forgive my mother for her failures as my mother. These failures were often exquisitely painful to me and left me with a residue of anger so powerful that it took me two decades to retool. In learning to deal with that anger, I have had to learn to locate its source, to mute its force, and to reuse the energy more profitably; but, of course, you did not benefit from any of this until well beyond the time when memory might have muted the harshness. During our talk, I found myself awed by the courage it took for you to begin and doggedly persevere at a conversation I could not make easy for you. I was also relieved that you had found the courage to abandon the path of nonconfrontation in your relationships. I remember something my friend Eddie Feld said to me long ago during a conversation about a woman who was not able to process her grief at the death of her daughter. I was curious about his understanding of the grieving process and asked him what, in his experience, happens when people cannot confront the enormity of their pain or loss. "If it can't come out any other way, it will come out in the cells," he answered. "What does that mean?" I asked him in puzzlement. "That's what cancer is for some people," he replied gravely. "It's the body quite literally allowing the grief to expand." I've thought about Eddie's comment for years. The fact that I can acknowledge my admiration for your courage in confronting me should not cause you to underestimate the depth of my pain in hearing the things you had to say. I tried, insofar as I was able that day, to explain myself to you. Ultimately, however, some of our failings as parents are simply the failure of personality, or character, or maturity, or evolution. I will tell you now what I told you then. I have no way to lessen for you the pain you suffered in having been an acutely sensitive child in the hands of a strong and assertive mother. But I will tell you that always, always, I gave you the best that I had available to me at the time to give. And sometimes my best was simply not good enough. I'm sorry for that.

When the doctor told my mother that she had an incurable brain tumor, she asked him how long she had to live. "Six months at the outside," he replied. I watched my mother's face carefully and knew immediately that she had resolved herself to die with all possible speed. After the doctor left her hospital room, I tried to talk to her about the importance of fighting toward life. She would not listen to me and finally, in fury, I turned to the mother I loved with an intense yet critical devotion and said fiercely, "I forgave you my childhood. I forgave you the neglect and the moments of abuse. But if you die without considering the possibility of fighting to live, may God be my witness when I swear to you that I will never forgive you for as long as I live." She looked directly at me and then away again, and said simply, "I can't. There's nothing I can do." She died two weeks later. It took me ten years to realize how unfair I was to my mother that day. Sometimes, even in a relationship where we are the child, there comes a time to act like an adult. Instead of allowing myself to be overwhelmed by my own impending loss, why could I not have tried to understand that day what it must have felt like to be my mother—a fifty-three-year-old woman who had just been told that she had six months left to live.

Noam, you have always been one of the most loyal people I know, and I want you to know that that quality is a family trait that goes back many generations. In my generation, Cousin Robin and Cousin Richard are the two who exemplify this most strongly. In Cousin Robin, this loyalty is particularly poignant, since our family was never accepting of Cousin Robin, whose personal style is different from the rest of us. But Cousin Robin taught me something about loyalty and generosity of spirit that I've never forgotten. When my mother refused to fight her tumor diagnosis, besides being infuriated with her, I devised a strategy I thought might galvanize her. I bought her a needlepoint to work on. I told her I wanted her to make it into a *tallit* bag for your Bar Mitzvah—which was, at that time, eleven years away. For the first time since she had heard the prognosis, I saw her eyes refocus on the living as she actually began to work on that needlepoint. She worked on it for a week, finished four rows of it, and died. I couldn't bear to see the needlepoint and put it away after the funeral. Three years later, Robin's mother, Aunt Miriam, asked me for the needlepoint. I dug it out from the top of the closet and gave it to her without a word, thankful to have it and its unfinished memories out of my life forever. Eight years later, a month before your Bar Mitzvah, Cousin Robin drove into New York and called to ask if she could come by. I was surprised to hear from her, since I hadn't seen her in years, but invited her to coffee. When she arrived, she obviously felt awkward and wordlessly handed me a paper bag. Inside was the needlepoint—which she had spent years finishing. I couldn't then, nor can I now, really thank Robin for the fullness of a heart that decided to give me the gift of my mother's presence at my son's Bar Mitzvah.

Kayla, you once asked me what the word *mensch* meant. I struggled to define its meaning, but I always meant to tell you this story by way of explanation. About a month after my mother died, you, who were then four years old, told me you had a headache. I called Dr. Gribetz's office and explained to the secretary that I needed to bring my daughter in on an extreme emergency. We arrived at Dr. Gribetz's office and the flustered secretary showed us into an examining room. Dr. Gribetz, you may recall, does not suffer fools gladly, and asked me curtly about the nature of the emergency. I explained, quite calmly, that you had a headache, which I thought might be a brain tumor. Dr. Gribetz, without raising an eyebrow or uttering any comment at all, turned to you to begin the examination. About ten minutes later, he asked me to shut the lights to the room so that he could look into the pupils of your eyes. When the lights were out, he turned toward me and asked conversationally, "Did I hear that your mother died recently?" "Yes," I replied noncommittally. "Brain tumor?" he pursued with a certain sympathy. "Yes," I gulped around the lump that had suddenly appeared in my throat. "Well, you can relax about this one," he said, indicating you. "She's fine—no sign of a brain tumor. And you needn't worry anymore. From now on, I'll keep an eye out for it." With that promise from Dr. Gribetz, I never again worried about you developing a brain tumor, and I never forgot what a mensch he was to me.

My family believed that one should never let anyone say anything complimentary about a child lest this bring the child to the attention of the Evil One.

Twenty-five years ago, my brother, Mark, went to my mother's school to drop off some papers. He stood quietly at the back of her classroom (she taught fourth grade) until she was free, and noticed a few students whispering together nearby. Shortly afterward, my mother dismissed the class for recess and turned to greet Mark, who remarked to her wryly, "Some things never change. Whenever I got into trouble for whispering, I always got sent to the back of the room too." "Not at all," replied my mother. "The students who sit in the back of the room in my class are my top students—the ones who can be trusted to work on their own. That's what the whispering was about." "What then do you do with problem students?" asked my brother in some surprise. "I move them up front closer to me," she replied with a smile. "They're the ones who need me the most."

Kayla, I've always thought that I raised you in a nonhomogenous world, but it wasn't until I opened the café that I learned how truly homogenous our world was. Danny, the manager of the café I own, is a Muslim from Egypt. I've come to understand, in the two years he has worked for me, how profoundly different are his and my backgrounds and cultural values. He sends money back to Egypt regularly to support his parents. I commented to him once that I admire the fact that he does this but that such financial support would be unheard of in our family, and in the Jewish community in which I was raised. Indeed, I explained, to Danny's evident astonishment, my father would feel himself to be a failure if he, as an adult, required the financial help of one of his children. Danny found this incomprehensible but, without my knowing it, tested out the information one day on my father when he visited me at the café. "What would happen," asked Danny of Dad, "if you needed money in your old age?" "Why, I suppose I would go to Sharon. But I would feel terrible to have to do it!" replied my father, to Danny's surprise. Danny and I have spent many months revisiting this topic, all the while exploring the differences in our cultural upbringings. We are each fascinated by the underlying assumptions in the other's culture, and I, who have always honestly believed that people are basically similar, understand how limited has been my vision of the world.

My brother, Mark, tried to make me understand exactly this point years before I ever met Danny. Many years ago, upon my arrival for a visit in Israel, Mark met me at Ben-Gurion Airport and inquired how my flight had been. I commented that the flight had been fine but that I always found myself exasperated by the lack of civility of Israelis in the passport-control lines at the airport. Why could the airport manager not organize normal lines to eliminate people shoving and pushing their way ahead? Mark tried to explain both the lines and the whole country to me, but when I argued with him, he finally exploded in exasperation, "You, my dear, seem to think that Israel is located somewhere in the West—probably near Chicago. It is not. It is located in the Middle East and *nothing* about the Middle East is Western. If you want to truly enjoy the time you spend here, you will have to give up your Western expectations and understand that this is a very different society from the one you left. It may look sophisticated or technologically adept, but don't be fooled into believing that it is Western." I did not really understand what he was trying to say to me at the time, but we've had the same conversation now for more than a decade and as I spend more and more time in Israel each year, I am able to probe deeper into Israeli society. I am learning that Western norms and Middle Eastern norms are, just as Mark said years ago, vastly different. Lately, I've been trying to work on learning not to judge which of those norms are "better."

My aunt Miriam is a role model for all of us on the slow and steady method of reaching a goal. She always knows where she's going and what she has to accomplish in order to get there, and yet I've never seen her ruffled or overwhelmed. This is a wonderful quality.

My zaydee (grandfather) used to say that if a man works a day, he is entitled to a day's pay. He meant that it is not right to delay paying workmen when they finish their job. This means nothing to you now, but be careful of this when you get older.

Cousin Stevie told me that he once asked Zaydee what made him decide to leave Poland and come to America. Zaydee replied in the following way: "You know I was a peddler in Poland. I would travel around with all my goods to the remote farms near my town of Mezritch and I was able to scrape out a small living selling things to the farmers. Many of my customers were not Jewish, and since I was a friendly fellow, I became friendly with them. One day, I was visiting the farm of a Polish farmer whom I liked. This man loved his wife and, as a special gift for her, had spent five years saving up animal pelts so he could make her a fur coat. One day, three Cossacks on horseback, carrying guns, rode up to his farm while I was there. They were not interested in me but pointed instead to the man's wife and said, 'Give us the coat.' The farmer stared at them in disbelief and laughed scornfully, replying, 'Give you the coat! I saved pelts for five years to make her that coat! I will not give you her coat!' " Zaydee paused reflectively and then continued the story. "I saw that the Polish farmer did not understand what the Jew already knew. And I liked this man. So I gathered all my courage and said to the Cossacks, 'One moment, please,' and I took the man aside. I said to him, 'Listen. You don't understand. These men are Cossacks. They are carrying guns. They want your wife's coat. If you love your wife, you'll make her a new coat and give them this coat. Life is too precious, and these Cossacks are serious.' The farmer turned wordlessly, removed the coat from his wife, and handed it to the Cossacks, who turned their horses around and left laughing. I knew that day," said Zaydee, "that it was time to leave Poland."

My zaydee used to eat a bowl of hot soup at every meal.

Before eating bread, my mother used to cut off the end of the loaf and throw it away. She learned this custom from her parents, who were worried that dough had not been taken before baking (*lehafrish* challah) according to the Jewish custom.

Cousin Stevie recently told me the reason Zaydee, whose name was Joe Finkelstein, appeared as Wolf Finkelstein on the passenger manifest for the SS *Polonia* in October 1928, when he arrived in America. Passports were very hard to come by in those days, so Joe's brother Wolf, who had already arrived in America a year earlier, sent his passport back to Poland for reuse by his brother Joe. Some years later, my grandfather, by now a U.S. citizen, decided to change his name legally back to his real name, Joe, and appeared before a New York judge to petition for a name change. "Why do you want to change your first name?" inquired the woman judge in some surprise, since it was more common to change a last name. "Lady Judge," replied my grandfather gravely, "are you married?" "Yes, I am," replied the judge in some amusement. "Well, if you weren't married and you wanted to get married," pursued my grandfather laboriously, "would you want to go out with a man named 'Wolf'?" "I see your point," replied the judge, with a twinkle in her eye. "Petition granted. And good luck with your marital plans!"

My zaydee was a *baal tefilah* (a leader of religious services) who often led services on the High Holidays at our synagogue in Providence. One year, he planned to be out of town for the High Holidays and told the synagogue leadership they would have to hire someone else for the services. The synagogue hired another *baal tefilah*, but at the last minute, my grandfather's plans changed and he stayed in town for the holidays.

Zaydee went to our synagogue the first evening of Rosh Hashanah and the new *baal tefilah* led the services. The next morning, when Zaydee arrived at the synagogue, the new *baal tefilah* came up to him just as he was taking his seat and, with tears in his eyes, begged Zaydee to take over and lead the services. "I wouldn't consider it," answered my grandfather. "You were hired and you have to finish the job." "I can't," answered the man. "I can see that the congregation does not want me. They want you. I will give you the salary they promised me, only you must lead services." "I won't take the job away from you," responded Zaydee firmly. "Just begin and everything will be fine." "No," answered the man. "In order to be the leader, one must be *merutzeh ha-kol* [literally, "wanted by all"]. I am not *merutzeh;* you are. And so you are obligated to lead." With that, Zaydee rose to his feet, went to the *bimah* (leader's podium), and began the services. After the holidays were over, the congregation sent Zaydee the money they had paid him in previous years to lead the services. He sent the money to the other *baal tefilah.*

In the story I just told you, I knew that Zaydee had given away the money paid to him that year, but it wasn't until after he died that I found out that in all the years my zaydee was paid to lead services for different congregations, he *never* kept the money. He always gave it away to a school.

My grandfather had a deep and old fear of hunger. For all the years that I knew him, I never knew his table to be without a loaf of bread on it.

Uncle Davey (may he rest in peace) used to make me laugh when he claimed that Jews were so poor when he was a child in Europe that Jewish housewives had to figure out how to create an entire Sabbath menu from one scrawny chicken. Here, according to Uncle Davey, is how they did it. They created a first course called fricassee by stewing the feet of the chicken and serving it over rice. The second course consisted of soup made from the chicken, accompanied by the neck and gizzards. The main course consisted, of course, of the chicken that had been stewed in the soup, and this was accompanied by *helzel*— stuffed neck skin of the chicken. Thank God, he used to say, that none had thought to devise a chicken cake; otherwise, that's what would have ended the meal.

Aunt Clara (whose Yiddish name was Kayla, and for whom you are named) believed strongly in one of our two famous family mottoes: You learn only from your mistakes (the second motto being You can trust only your enemies to tell you the truth). This latter belief led her to freely criticize anyone in her immediate vicinity in the genuine hope of improving their character (which, unfortunately, was only an occasionally successful strategy). It happened one day that Aunt Clara's son Sonny was having fun wrestling with his father, Uncle Ralph, when his hand slipped and he accidentally bloodied his father's nose. They came into the house and Uncle Ralph said, "Clara,

I need ice." Aunt Clara took in the situation immediately and said tersely, "Ralph, go into our bedroom and I'll bring you the ice. Sonny, go to your room and wait for me there." Then she retrieved the ice from the freezer and brought it to Ralph. As she handed it to him, she began to rail at him, "Ralph, how stupid can you be?! A grown man wrestling with a child? You could have seriously hurt him, God forbid! Use some common sense!" Then she left the room and went into Sonny's room. "Sonny," she began, "what kind of a fool are you? Your father is an old man. Thank God you only bloodied his nose! You could, God forbid, have seriously hurt him!" Sonny, who had already overheard his mother berating his father, commented, "Ma, I know you just yelled at Pa. And I also know that we can't both be wrong!" Aunt Clara gave him a measured look and responded without a trace of humor, "Of course you can both be wrong! Whichever person I'm talking to is always the one who's wrong!"

Thinking back, Uncle Ralph's habits seem strange to me now, but they didn't when I was a child. When my mother wanted to talk to Uncle Ralph (who was an extremely successful businessman in Rhode Island), she would go to the Dunkin' Donuts on Elmwood Avenue at 4:30 A.M. Everyone in the family and the business community knew that he could be found there at that time any weekday morning, meeting with his accountants, and lawyers, and other family members or businesspeople who needed to talk to him.

Sonny is absolutely the most frugal person I know. I have never known him to deliberately waste or ruin anything that could be salvaged—except once. This is what happened. His father, Uncle Ralph, sometimes used to take perverse ideas into his mind and would stubbornly adhere to them no matter what evidence was presented otherwise. Once, he decided that one of his daughters had tried to cheat him out of some land he owned. He announced that he was changing his will and that she and her family would be cut out of their inheritance. The daughter herself, and then the other siblings, tried to talk to their father to explain the misunderstanding, but Uncle Ralph refused to listen. Finally, Sonny called his father at home and said he would be there to visit shortly. When he arrived, his father was watching television, sitting very close to the screen. Sonny began to try to explain the misunderstanding, and in response, Uncle Ralph leaned forward and turned up the volume on the television set. Sonny tried to speak once more and Uncle Ralph responded the same way. Sonny turned around and went downstairs to his car. He removed the tire iron from his trunk, reentered the living room, and calmly smashed in the television set. "Do I have your attention now?" he asked his father pleasantly. Thereafter they were able to clear up the misunderstanding.

My grandmother once went to Elizabeth, New Jersey, to discuss a family problem with her youngest brother, Abe, for whom she nourished a fierce and thoroughly uncritical devotion. Abe's wife, Sarah, served them both lunch and then sat down at the table to listen to the conversation. My grandmother turned to Sarah and politely asked her to leave, since she wanted to discuss private family matters with her brother. Sarah, no shrinking violet herself, announced that as Abe's wife she was part of the family and entitled to stay. "No, Sarah," responded my grandmother gravely. "You are not family. Family is *blood* relation. You are a *bed* relation." Sarah got up wordlessly, left the room, and never forgot the incident. As an old woman, Sarah, who survived both Abe and my grandmother, was fond of quoting the story and often referred to herself as a "bed relation." There was a certain wry satisfaction in the way she said it. That very wryness has made me wonder, in the ensuing years, whether my grandmother was incredibly insensitive and disrespectful, or whether she acknowledged some tacit truth with which Sarah concurred that day when she left the room.

When Aunty Sarah told me the story of how my grandmother Chai-Raizel disparagingly referred to her as a "bed relation," I realized for the first time that the family has always had a profound belief that blood family is the only reliable thing in the world. This is wrong, but sometimes, despite myself, it feels true. That is why my closest friends are Sonny, Mark, Debby, and lately, Richard—all relatives. For the other close relationships in my life, I gave myself permission to transform Annie, Rina, Kathy, Judy, and Michael into more sisters and brothers and this allowed me to be friends with them. I think this is something many of us do—allowing our friendships to deepen so that our friends become a part of our families.

Aunty Sarah had a caustic tongue and never minced words when she had something to say. When I was a child, she frightened me, but I grew to love her as I got older. As an adult, I used to visit her every few weeks and drive her wherever she needed to go—on shopping expeditions, on charitable excursions, or to visit friends. One thing I admired tremendously about her was this: whether I had taken her to visit a very famous revered rabbi or a shopkeeper's assistant (we visited both), she treated each person exactly the same.

Aunty Sarah taught me that it is possible to listen to the voice underneath the words to understand how deeply you are loved.

Aunty Sarah used to turn up her nose in derision when someone in the family was honored by an organization to which they had given a lot of money. She believed that charity, even large amounts of it, should be given quietly and anonymously.

In America, charity has become big business. I often think of Aunt Clara, who was a very wealthy but especially frugal person. She gave generously to the Rhode Island Jewish Federation each year until the year she happened to be looking out her window and noticed the federation solicitor getting out of a cab in front of her house. He came into the house and launched into his solicitation, only to be told by Aunt Clara that if she herself was not ashamed to take a bus, he, who was, after all, using Jewish communal funds, could also save the cab fare and take buses too!

Cousin Lenny was tremendously committed to the notion of family. After his divorce, he was determined that his children—Robin, Lauren, and Bobby—would know and feel close to the extended family. For that reason, when his children were young, he would rent a boat and sail with them to Rhode Island, where he would pick up whomever of the cousins were around that summer. At Lenny's shiva, I was startled to hear how many cousins had memories of those summer jaunts, and how many lives became entwined because of them. Cousin Richard continues the tradition today by organizing family ski vacations with whomever he can cajole into joining him. Our house in Great Barrington has often served as a family gathering spot for the various cousins—a practice which delights me.

When I was a child, my zaydee used to tell me stories about Papa Abraham and Mama Sarah. The stories he told me about incidents that had happened to them in their lives were so real that I felt as if I had known them when they all lived together in Europe. It wasn't until I began school that I learned that the people Zaydee had been telling me about were not relatives but the biblical figures Abraham and Sarah.

Kayla and Noam, you grew up in a world that had a vast tolerance for different religious standards. I know you think that such tolerance is the norm in religious homes, but that is not true. It was my zaydee who taught me everything I know about being both religious and tolerant. After my first book was published, I was invited back to my Orthodox Jewish day school in Rhode Island to speak. I myself was no longer Orthodox, and I agreed to speak with no small amount of trepidation. I knew that, in the course of my speech, the fact that I was no longer Orthodox would emerge and I assumed my zaydee would be in the audience and would be devastated by this. Sure enough, during the question-and-answer period, I was asked many questions about my personal religious practices. I talked freely about my feminism and egalitarianism, and, in answer to one of the questions, told those present that I would be leading the Kol Nidre prayer on Yom Kippur for our minyan (this being the most solemn prayer of the liturgy, my revelation was met by a collective gasp from the audience). After the speech, Zaydee invited me to have tea with him at his home. I knew what was coming, and sure enough, he asked me many, many questions about my minyan, where we davened (led services), what our religious practices were, how I had learned to lead services, etc. He never criticized me; he merely asked neutral questions. My answer to the question of how we *lain*ed (chanted) without a Torah scroll interested him (our minyan did not have enough money to buy a Torah scroll—which in those days cost $10,000—so we used a Bible and simply *lain*ed from the book instead of a scroll). I returned to New York, and Zaydee called me a week later to say he would be driving in to visit me overnight the following day. He arrived and, having unloaded his luggage from the car, sat with me over a cup of tea and asked me further questions about my minyan. Finally, having circled around where he wanted to go, he asked me how I planned to lead the Kol Nidre service without knowing the *nusach* (liturgical chant). I explained that a friend had taught me the *nusach*. Zaydee replied: "No, Sherelleh. Your friend taught you his *nusach*. I came here to teach you ours." He then spent the next half hour recording on tape his family Kol Nidre *nusach* for me and that is the *nusach* I use to this day. When we had finished, he went into the den and came out carrying a Torah scroll, which he kissed and then handed to me. I stared at him in shock and he merely said quietly, "We Jews do not *lain* from a Bible; we *lain* from a *sefer* Torah. This is for you. Guard it." I doubt that you can understand yet how extraordinary a gesture it was for an Orthodox man to teach his granddaughter how to lead Kol Nidre and entrust to her a *sefer* Torah as his gift of faith.

Know where you
are going . . .

M oney is more important than you think it is now but less important than it will feel at those times that you're strapped for it.

About money, my mother taught me that "it's very easy to go up but very hard to come down." By this she meant that to increase your level of spending and improve your lifestyle can be comfortable and fun but to need to reduce your level of spending can be painful and difficult. Her solution, then, was to live as frugally as possible so as never to face the problem. I am of the opinion that my mother erred in this. There is an important life lesson in understanding in a deep way what it is we need in our lives and making sure that those things that we need are the things we manage to acquire. The trick in life is not to be suckered into believing that other people's material needs are your own—and this can happen with clothes, vacations, houses, education, cars, anything at all.

My mother bought almost anything if it was on sale. I have learned from this that it is better to buy the one thing you truly love.

Everyone I've ever met, and I mean *everyone*—no matter how wealthy—exercises certain frugalities in his life. It is often interesting and illuminating to discover what a person's particular frugalities are.

My friend Leah, the psychiatrist, told me that when she has to hire a nanny or housekeeper, she likes to hire someone who was the oldest child in their own family, since she believes the oldest child is the one parents unwittingly train to be the most responsible.

Find a teacher. Just as Sonny has been such a person for me, you will do well to find yourself someone who can be a role model for you in your life. When you do, be careful not to follow blindly. Just hear the voice of someone you respect when you have a decision to make.

Sonny told me never to lend money to a family member. Either give it as a gift or don't give it, but don't lend it. If you lend money to a family member who is not able to repay you, you'll inevitably have bad feelings about the loss and eventually you may end up losing a family member. That's a bigger loss than the money could ever be.

Sonny has taught me, over the years, the habit of asking the question, "What am I really afraid of? What is the worst thing that can happen if I do ————?" This is an invaluable tool in helping you to face your fears and devise strategies to minimize your risk.

I've always been very close to my brother, Mark. When Mark married Debby, I rejoiced in his very evident happiness, and I also secretly worried that my relationship with my brother would be supplanted by his with his new wife. I did not, at that time, understand the wisdom of the woman he had chosen. Upon her marriage to my brother, Debby opened up her heart and established a separate place for me there too. Only a very wise and very generous person would have had the insight to do this.

For a long time after I married your father, I felt alienated from his family because I misinterpreted who they were. I judged their behavior and responses by my family's standards. This is a bad thing to do. When you marry someone, you have to enter their family system and suspend judgments based on your own family's standards.

When people used to say enviously of someone, *"Sie hut a sach mazel!"* (literally, "She has a lot of luck!"), my mother used to answer, "A person makes their own *mazel*." This is true. We can, by force of will and sheer determination, make something happen that others believe can't happen. It doesn't always work this way, but if you believe deeply in something and are willing to work tirelessly toward it, you can often make miracles.

Your grandfather, Zaydee-in-the-hat, is the embodiment of the verse in Ethics of the Fathers, "Who is the wealthy person? The one who is content with his portion." My father has the most balanced view of life of anyone I've ever met.

All my life, whenever I have asked my father for a favor, no matter how difficult or how inconvenient, he has, with deep pleasure and no questions, done it. This is a quality I cherish in my father.

My father said he never knew what a treasure he had in my mother until after she died. I often think to myself how unutterably sad this was—for him and for her.

Noam, our family has a remarkably strong work ethic, which I can tell you inherited by your performance at the first job you ever held—as a computer consultant at CTS Group. You, who could not get yourself out of bed before 11:00 A.M. on any non-work morning, were never, ever late getting to work. I found this small fact absolutely astonishing but realized you had inherited the family's strong feelings about work. Uncle Ralph had the strongest work ethic of anyone I've ever met, and he was uncompromising in passing it down to his grandchildren. Two of those grandchildren, Richard Shuster and Alan Harlam, worked one summer moving pallets at Cast Products—which was a new business that Ralph had recently acquired. No one at the plant knew that Richard and Alan were the owner's grandchildren. Indeed, no one at the plant that summer knew yet who the new owner was. After working there some weeks, Richard and Alan became friendly with the woman packer who worked near them. She confided in them one day that she thought the new management was terrible. "Why do you feel that way?" asked Richard in surprise. "Just look at the old man they hired to load coils on that pallet!" she retorted indignantly, pointing to their grandfather, Ralph. As the new owner, Ralph was adhering to the custom he had of coming into a new business at 6:00 A.M. and working alongside the other workers until 5:00 P.M. "I'll bet they're paying him three dollars an hour and he must be sixty years old if he's a day!" she continued disgustedly. "They could at least have given him a desk job!"

My family believes in giving charity every time you do a business deal. That means whether you make *or lose* money, you must set aside money for charity.

Noam, it can sometimes feel silly not to cut corners when the ways and means are presented to you, but it is always better to be meticulous in your business dealings. Once it happened that I was selling a house I owned in the Berkshires to a wealthy man. He called me up sometime after I had accepted his offer and asked me to come to his office to meet with him about a matter of some delicacy. I met him later that week and he explained that he wanted to pay me part of the purchase price of the house in actual cash (like hundred-dollar bills). I thought about it, thanked him politely, and declined the offer. He was momentarily quite nonplussed and then his brow cleared. "Honey," he said, leaning toward me earnestly (you can imagine, I know, how his calling me "honey" endeared him to me), "do you have a business adviser—you know, someone you could call who could explain what I mean to you?" By now thoroughly enjoying myself, I replied earnestly that my cousin Sonny, himself a very successful businessman, was the one I always turned to when I didn't understand things. "Perfect!" replied the buyer, with evident satisfaction. "Call him now and he can explain it to you." I called Sonny from the man's office and explained the offer that the buyer had made to me. Sonny listened carefully and then responded in the following way: "When I first got into business, someone approached me with the same offer." "What did you do?" I asked interestedly. "I called my father," he replied. "And what did Uncle Ralph say?" I pursued. Sonny said: "Ralph said to me, 'Sonny, this is really a very simple problem. You have only to answer this question: Do you like to eat or do you like to sleep?' " I pondered for a moment and asked Sonny, "And which was it?" Sonny chastised me gently: "You know me well enough by now to know that I like to sleep." I thanked Sonny and got off the phone. Turning to the buyer, I shook hands with him and explained apologetically, "I'm sorry. My cousin feels the same way I do. All of us like to sleep."

When I first got into real estate, I did not do it in half measures. I bought three brownstone apartment buildings with a total of twenty-four apartments. I did not know the first thing about managing apartment buildings, handling tenants, or negotiating the rent-stabilization and rent-control systems in New York City. Within two months, I was drowning in tenant problems. I realized in despair that I was a terrible manager and an even worse businesswoman, and that I should sell the buildings and get out of business immediately. I called Cousin Sandy, whose family was in the real estate business in New York, and told him I wanted to sell the three buildings I had bought two months earlier. "I'll send my cousin Moish over to talk with you," he said. When Moish arrived, I showed him the buildings and told him everything that was going on. He asked many questions and I answered as honestly as I could. Finally, he said to me, "Sharon, I'd be happy to buy your buildings from you, but I want to be honest with you. There's no reason in the world for you to sell them." "Why not?" I asked in astonishment. "I don't know the first thing about managing apartment buildings and, more importantly, the tenant situation is out of control." "Do you play chess?" asked Moish, in what I considered to be the silliest non sequitur I had ever heard. "Sure I play chess," I answered. "Why is that relevant?" "Because," he answered, "with you, everything is personal. You are responding to your tenants' provocation as if they were deliberately trying to wound you. Keep in mind that when a new landlord comes into the picture, there's always some reshuffling and posturing that happens. But none of it is directed at you personally." "It's not?" I asked in amazement. "Of course not," he answered. "For the tenants, it's only a chess game. And that is how you have to begin to see business. First they make a move. Then you make a move. That's the whole deal." To this day, I have no idea why the chess analogy clicked for me. Somehow it allowed me to depersonalize the tenant maneuvers, make the required repairs, and restabilize the situation. And, as it happened, I'm lucky Moish talked me out of selling him those buildings, because I turned out to be a pretty good businesswoman.

Few decisions in life need to be made immediately. It's often better to wait a few days before making a decision.

Kayla, you have chosen to concentrate on your intellectual interests up to now, but I believe that, should you ever choose to use it, you could summon a pretty sharp business instinct. I know you don't know this to be true about yourself, but I have watched you ask questions, and I know that the possibility lurks inside you—along with other possibilities that you may choose to explore as you grow. It is important to accept the full breadth of who you are and not close yourself down to all of your possibilities. It took me many years to uncover my own interest in business. I was trained to be a teacher and a writer and I had no idea that an interest in business lurked inside me. In the course of uncovering and accepting my attraction to business, I learned that while I find business incredibly interesting, I myself have no more business acumen than anyone else. What I bring to the table in a business deal is a formidable amount of energy and very little fear. In life, people who have real energy and are not hesitant or fearful to use it often experience two things: they are exploited by those with less energy or more fear, and, in business, they often receive disproportionate rewards. I don't understand why this latter is true, but I know that it is so.

Because I own real estate, many people call me for advice on matters of real estate. I used to spend a lot of time on the phone with these people until I realized that, more often than not, they wanted approbation for what they were planning to do rather than actual feedback on their ideas. One person for whom this was not true was my friend Jerry. He called me about ten years ago and said he wanted to buy a home in the

$200,000 range in the Salisbury area of Connecticut and wanted advice on how to proceed. We agreed that his budget might be overly modest for that area, but he was quite firm that this was his real price range. I then told him to call the local brokers and see everything in the area that he could in the price range up to $225,000. Some weeks later, he called me back discouraged and said, "I did as you suggested and saw *everything* in the price range up to two hundred and twenty-five thousand dollars. There was very little on the market and what was there was absolutely awful—in the middle of a highway or falling to bits. What do I do now?" he asked. I replied, "Now go back to the Realtor you liked working with the best and tell him that you want to see real estate in a price range up to three hundred and twenty-five thousand dollars. Tell the Realtor, though, that this time you want to see real estate that's a tough sell for one reason or another—in other words, distressed merchandise." Jerry was dubious but game. Within two months, he had found a horribly designed house complete with indoor pool on a beautiful piece of land. The asking price was $300,000 and Jerry bought it for slightly more than $200,000.

I don't know why this is so, but I can buy a $3 million piece of real estate without a shred of indecision. What I can't do is buy a pair of shoes that cost more than $70.

Lots of people speak authoritatively without the necessary expertise to back it up. Be wary of such people.

There will come a time in your life when you will no doubt encounter anti-Semitism. I've encountered my share and, no matter how often it's happened, I've always found it disconcerting. As far as I can tell, there are two different kinds of anti-Semitism, and, for me, one kind is easier to deal with than the other. I'll tell you two stories to explain what I mean. The first is the story about the brownstone you grew up in. I decided to buy a house in Manhattan when you were a newborn, Kayla, since our two-bedroom apartment was beginning to feel quite cramped. I looked in the real estate ads of the *New York Times* and saw an ad for a brownstone for sale for $65,000. I called the owner and the next day, your father and I went to see it. I was twenty-six years old and knew nothing about buying a house. The owner met us at the door and showed us the house, and at the end of the tour, I turned to her, shook her hand solemnly, and said, "We'll take it." (I had some vague notion that the price for a house was like the price of a dress at Macy's.) I called your great-grandfather, Hyman Goldstein, who was a gentle, nonaggressive, fair, and honorable lawyer, and asked if he would serve as the attorney for the transaction. He was delighted that we were buying a home and readily agreed. Both we and the seller signed a contract of sale and I went back to see the house with my friend Michael Paley later that same week. As I was being led through the house for the second time, the seller turned to me and said musingly, "Strassfeld . . . Strassfeld . . . is that a German name?" I was absorbed in taking room measurements and answered distractedly that, yes, my father-in-law had lived in Germany (he had also lived in a whole series of other countries while he was fleeing Europe, but I didn't bother explaining that to her). "Good," responded the seller with evident satisfaction in her voice. "I was afraid you were Jewish, since the Jews have been buying up houses around here lately." I was stunned and put down my tape measure to turn to her. "By the way," I said, trying to peer through the red haze that had suddenly appeared before my eyes, "I am not sure if I introduced you to my friend. This is Rabbi Michael Paley." Without another word, the seller turned and walked out the front door, pointedly holding it open for us to leave. Later that day, I got a call from Zaydee Goldstein. "I just received a call from the seller's attorney," he began. "It seems they've decided not to sell you the house." "Really?" I asked. "Can they do that?" "Not really," replied the ever gentle Zaydee. "But you don't want to have a fight. And they'll send you your deposit back so you can start to look around for another house," he added. "Zaydee," I said, "give me the name and phone number of the seller's lawyer. I'll give him a call myself so you won't have to be bothered with this." Within five minutes, I had the seller's attorney on the line. I said to him in as neutral a tone as I could muster, "Your client is an anti-Semite who doesn't want to sell us her house because we're Jewish. I want you to know that I am not a person who goes around issuing threats. So when I tell you now that there is nothing I won't do to own that house, you can regard that as my personal commitment. And you can believe it." To my surprise, he did not comment on a single thing I had said. He merely said he would convey my message to his client and hung up. An hour later, my phone rang. Zaydee Goldstein was on the line. "I just got a call from the seller's attorney," he began, clearly puzzled. "The seller must be quite indecisive. The attorney tells me that his client has just called to say that she has changed her mind and she will sell you the house." "Thank you for calling, Zaydee," I replied politely, and hung up the receiver. That was the first time I ever faced down an anti-Semite, and it felt damn good.

The other kind of anti-Semitism is the kind that invites collusion on the part of the Jew and I find it particularly detestable. I'll tell you what happened to me in East Hampton, New York, one summer to explain what I mean. I was looking at a piece of property with a very charming, wealthy, and urbane man who had changed his mind about developing the property himself and was now intending to sell it. In the course of spending the few hours it took to get to the property, see it, and drive back, we talked together about all sorts of things and eventually came to the subject of our children. I asked him what schools he was considering for his three-year-old son and he replied, "We had thought about Dalton and went to look at it, but then we decided it was too Jewish." I was incredibly offended, extremely curious about what he thought he was saying to me, and at a complete loss about how to respond—just as I've always been in situations where calling someone on their anti-Semitism (or antifeminism or racism) requires me to be directly confrontational in an otherwise casual social setting. If I confront directly, I risk putting myself into the category of all those "hypersensitive" Jews (angry women . . . whatever) who see anti-Semitism under every rock. Yet, to let the remark pass is to collude in the anti-Semitism itself. That dilemma is exactly why I detest people who are underhanded about their anti-isms. At least when it's out there as real hatred, I can get a handle on it and feel free to confront it with all the energy in my arsenal.

Someone besides the seller of our brownstone once wanted to get out of a business deal with me and I responded differently that time. This is what happened. A year after I bought our brownstone, I bought three other brownstones on the same block. After I bought those buildings, many of my friends called me to congratulate me on buying real estate and to ask me to let them know if I heard of another "good deal," since they too would be interested in buying property. Mrs. Rottenberg was the elderly woman who owned the seventeen-unit apartment building next to mine. She used to sweep her stoop and the sidewalk gutter in front of her building every morning, and we would stop to chat together whenever we saw each other. One day, shortly after I bought the three buildings near hers, she stopped me and said to me, "*Nu,* so you bought Avi's buildings. If you wanted to buy a building, why didn't you tell me—I would have sold you mine!" "I didn't know you were interested in selling," I said. "Why not?" she replied. "Younger, I'm not getting." "Don't worry, Mrs. Rottenberg," I replied. "I know you have a good, clean building. If you are ready to sell, I know a lot of people who have told me they're interested in buying. I'll help you find someone." I called the half-dozen people who had told me to keep an eye out for them. I actually brought two of them to see the building, but both people were clearly too intimidated to proceed. The others couldn't even be persuaded to look. After the second friend turned down the building, Mrs. Rottenberg called me up and asked me to come over. "Listen to me and take my advice," she said to me as soon as she saw me. "*You* buy my building. I guarantee you that this building will pay the tuition for Kayla's college education! It's a good building—a very fine building," she added coaxingly. I looked at her, sighed resignedly, and said, "Okay, Mrs. Rottenberg. I'll buy your building." So we went to contract the following week. Two days later, I got a call from Mrs. Rottenberg's nephew Jack, who himself owned many large apartment buildings. "She's changed her mind again," he said in a frantic tone of voice. "Every time she gets ready to sell, she backs down. Now, she's going to call you and tell you she doesn't want to sell anymore. But you got farther than anyone else, since she actually signed a contract with you. Just tell her that you'll sue her for specific performance and she'll back down." Jack, I knew, was only thinking about his aunt, worried about an eighty-year-old woman sweeping the stoop, vacuuming the hallways, and shoveling the snow. Nevertheless, I was not prepared to force someone whose whole life revolved around caring for her building to sell before she was ready. So I told Jack to leave it alone and his aunt and I would work something out together. Sure enough, Mrs. Rottenberg called me later that day. She asked me to come over and when I arrived, she told me firmly that she had changed her mind. "That's no problem," I answered calmly. "I'll go home and bring back the contract and you can give me back my down payment." "Good," she replied, relieved. I brought her back the contract and did not hear from her the rest of that day or the next. The third day, Jack called back. "I don't know what you did," he began, "but she's willing to sell the building." "I didn't actually do anything," I replied. "I just gave her the opportunity to get ready to sell in case she wanted to. And I guess she did." The sale went through; Mrs. Rottenberg moved to an apartment house for the elderly in Washington, where she was quite happy; and, twenty-five years later, I know that Mrs. Rottenberg was right. Darling Kayla, that building did indeed help send you through Brown University (and you, Noam, to Clark University!).

Never rent if you can buy.

Kayla, when you were a senior in high school, I made you an offer that you rejected. I found your dilemma an interesting one and the decision you reached at that time consistent with your values. You were accepted by Brown University and then offered an astonishing opportunity by another college—an all-expense-paid college education. I encouraged you to try the other school, although I believed you would be happiest at Brown. To counterbalance the choice, I made the following proposal to you: I would give you a check for $120,000 (the amount that a four-year education at Brown University was likely to cost me) on the day you graduated from the other institution. I saw the indecision in your eyes as you contemplated my offer for just a moment. Then you resolutely shook your head and told me that you were sure that Brown was the right intellectual community for you. I respect you for making that decision, even though I am not sure I would have made the same choice at your age. In the ensuing years, I have occasionally wondered what your decision will feel like to you as you look back on it later on in your life.

In life, when we are young, we believe that the whole world is open to us and anything that we want can happen. This is not true. What is true is that we get far fewer chances than we imagine and so it is important to grasp with both hands those that come our way. Kayla, you will understand this from the decision to choose Brown University over your other choice.

I did not do well by either of you in giving you messages about our financial situation. I know that as a young child, you, Kayla, were confused about what our resources were. I remember one poignant incident when you came home from kindergarten at Ramaz Lower School crying one day because each child had been asked to describe the apartment he lived in and you had had to shamefacedly confess that, unlike the other children, we lived in a brownstone. I tried, valiantly, to explain that many people would prefer to live in a one-family brown-stone than in an apartment building, but you remained dis-tressed and unconvinced. Noam, you had similar confusion about our situation, which lasted much longer than kinder-garten. Well into high school, you were mourning the fact that we weren't wealthy enough to buy you as many upgrades on your computer as you would have liked. I made some slight effort over the years to let you know that some of the financial decisions we made were "we choose not to" rather than "we can't" decisions, but you were never able to distinguish the two. I suppose I might as well confess that I believe unless chil-dren are one day going to inherit massive amounts of money or property for which they need to be trained in management (and you aren't), I don't think there's any point in talking to children too much about money. I figure most kids don't understand anyway, and if they're really interested, they'll let us know and we can educate that child as he is able to absorb the information. When you are adults, if you kids think you need to be wealthy, I expect that you will figure out how to get there.

My friend Judy Peck and I have spent many hours discussing the reasons why, despite the fact that I myself am not poor, I have a prejudice against rich people. She says this is not fair. But I believe that many rich people have a kind of subtle arrogance and assumption of entitlement that I dislike.

On this subject, there is a story told about the Gerrer Rebbe that I have always enjoyed. The Gerrer Rebbe was concerned about the inequities among his Hasidim between those who had money and those who didn't. Accordingly, the rabbi created a series of sumptuary laws designed to protect those with limited means and spare them embarrassment. One of those laws limited the number of guests that families could invite to a wedding. Once a wealthy Hasid came to the Gerrer Rebbe and said, "You know that I am wealthy and have many friends and business associates. I would like you to waive your rule limiting the number of guests I can invite to my wedding." "If you are so wealthy," replied the Gerrer, "perhaps you can buy yourself another rebbe."

My friend Barry Holtz once called me the "kugel queen." He was referring to the fact that my cuisine was quite often eastern

European Jewish (stuffed cabbage, brisket, pot roast, *cholent,* kugel, latkes, etc.). From all of this array, you, Kayla, became a vegetarian with an emphasis on Mexican and Thai food, and you, Noam, eat mainly fried chicken and salami. Still, both of you used to love my potato kugel, which was actually my friend Judy Robbins's recipe. Judy makes the best potato kugel because she soaks about one-third of a leftover challah in the mixture of eggs, onions, and ground potatoes. She lets the challah get very soft and then stirs the wet challah dough throughout the potato kugel mix. This lightens the whole kugel so that it doesn't taste as heavy as traditional potato kugel can taste. Also, I oil the potato kugel pan with about 1/4 inch of oil and put it in a very hot oven (450 degrees). When the oil is sizzling hot, I add the raw kugel mixture and put it back in the very hot oven. Then I turn the oven down to 350 degrees and let the kugel cook until it's brown and crisp around the edges. Yummy.

My friend Ruthie Lindenbaum once said to me in utter seriousness, "I've been thinking a lot about men and trying to understand why they are so different from us. I've also been thinking a lot about the Creation story in the Bible. And I came to a very profound understanding about that story and men. You remember that the story says that God caused a deep sleep to fall over Adam and he removed a rib and created Eve?" "Yes," I answered. "Well," she continued triumphantly, "I suddenly realized that God took out other parts too and never told us about it!"

Men and women are profoundly different from one another in ways we neither of us fully understand.

The corollary to this is that men and women do not speak the same language or listen with the same hearing, so it is pointless to judge a man with a woman's ears.

Wolfe Kelman was a wise man and a charming raconteur. When you were quite young, Kayla, we were invited to Wolfe and Jackie's home for Shabbat dinner. Wolfe told the following story that night. During the sixties, it became chic for large corporations to invite scholars and thinkers to address their corporate managers. Noted theologian (and Wolfe's dear friend) Abraham Joshua Heschel was invited to be the scholar in residence at a meeting of AT&T executives. Heschel spoke that day about Judaism and Jewish values. When it came time for questions and answers, one of the executives raised his hand and asked, "Rabbi Heschel, you talked about the Jewish notion of forgiveness during your speech and what I want to know is this: How come you people can't forgive Hitler and move on from the war, which was over almost twenty years ago?" The room grew hushed waiting for Heschel's response. Heschel was silent for a moment and then replied, "Gentlemen of the

AT&T. I would like to answer the very interesting question you pose by telling you a story that happened a generation ago to a very great Jewish scholar whose name was Reb Chaim of Brisk. Reb Chaim was once traveling by train back to his home-town of Brisk. Into the same train car entered three Jewish peasants. They set up a game of cards and looked over at Reb Chaim, who had immersed himself in a holy book and was oblivious to their presence. They called out to him boisterously to demand his participation as a fourth in their card game. Reb Chaim, remaining oblivious to all but his book, did not respond. The peasants began to taunt Reb Chaim and when he still did not respond, they grew angry, converged on him, picked him up, and threw him and his book out of the car. Reb Chaim silently picked up his belongings and moved to the next train car, where he again immersed himself in his holy studies. When the Brisk train stop arrived, Reb Chaim descended from the train and was greeted, as befitted his status, by the entire town, who had come to welcome home their rebbe. The three peasants also descended at Brisk and were appalled to discover who it was they had insulted. They tried to speak to Reb Chaim on the spot but were not able to because the townspeople sur-rounded the rebbe to escort him home. The next day, the peasants went to Reb Chaim's house to meet with him. They begged his forgiveness, saying that they had had no idea who he was and would never have insulted him if they had known. Reb Chaim replied gently, 'Gentlemen, I know that this is true. Had you known me as Reb Chaim, you would never have thrown me out of the car. The one that you insulted, then, was the poor peasant Jew that you thought me to be. And on that Jew's account, I cannot forgive you, since I am not he. You will have to find that peasant and beg his forgiveness.' " Heschel gazed silently at the audience. "Gentlemen," he said finally, "I myself was here in America during the war. My daughter was safe. My wife was safe. And since I and my loved ones were safe, I cannot be the one to forgive Hitler. For that, you will have to find the infants, the children, the husbands, the wives, the grandparents—those who were the victims. The ones who suffered are the only people who can extend forgiveness." It is twenty years since I heard Wolfe tell that story in Heschel's name and I can still hear Wolfe's deep and beautiful voice and see you, Kayla, curled up in your chair at his table listening silently to the story.

Shmuel Himelstein, in his book, tells another story about Reb Chaim of Brisk that I had heard long ago. Once a fire broke out in the town of Brisk and many homes burned to the ground. Reb Chaim's house was not harmed, and yet after the fire, he chose to sleep in the synagogue with those who had been left homeless. Leaders of the town came to Reb Chaim to ask him why he slept in the synagogue. Replied Reb Chaim, "I cannot sleep in my own bed when there are so many homeless. I will continue to sleep at the synagogue until all who were left homeless have a roof over their heads. If I stayed in my own home, it might take the community a long time to raise the money to rebuild the homes of all the homeless. But if the community knows that I too sleep in the synagogue until their work is done, the fund-raising will go much faster." When the last home was finally built, Reb Chaim moved back home.

If you want to do good for your community, do direct volunteer work. Don't sit on boards of organizations and convince yourself that you are doing real work. The real work is in the field, not in a boardroom.

My friend Michael Paley tells the story of officiating at the funeral of a woman who had died. As is customary, the immediate mourners—in this case the woman's husband and children—sat in the front row while other friends and relatives sat in the rows behind them. At the back of the room, Michael noticed a man sobbing quietly to himself throughout the funeral. Some days later, as Michael was about to get into his car in a parking lot, the same man approached him and introduced himself. "Would you have any time to talk with me now?" the man asked hesitantly, and in response, Michael invited the man into his car for a chat. "I find myself overwhelmed by grief at ———'s death," began the man. "This is a little awkward to tell a rabbi, but she and I were lovers for twenty years. Although she was never willing to break up her family to be with me, I never doubted that she loved me. In my mind, she was always my wife. My heart is broken, and yet I have no way to grieve since our relationship was secret, and I am not a family member." Michael responded, "From what you have just told me, we buried a member of your family three days ago. When a member of our family dies, we Jews have the custom to recite kaddish. You have the same right as any other mourner in the community to recite kaddish for the loss of a loved one, and I urge you to find a minyan where you can recite kaddish during the year of your mourning." I often think about that man. I think about how complicated and secret are the lives of many people, and about how lucky he is that he stumbled into Michael's wise and loving care when he was in pain.

My mother needed security in her life much more than I find I have needed in mine. She once offered to buy me a house in Providence, Rhode Island, if I would move back there and resume my teaching career (she was frightened of my more entrepreneurial side and longed for me to live near her and have a "steady paycheck"). I loved teaching in the years that I did it. But after five years, I felt that I had finished teaching and I was ready to start something new. I went from teaching, to writing, to real estate, to construction, to restaurants, to writing, to . . . I'm not sure where next. From this, I learned that it is not necessarily a good thing to believe that the career you choose when you are twenty-one is the same career you will be pursuing when you are forty-five. Sometimes it's time to move on to something new because you've finished what there is to do.

Don't be a snob. Interesting people exist in many different places. Among the more interesting people I know are Frank DeCrescenzo, my hairdresser; Esther Hautzig, a writer; Richard Shuster, a hedge fund manager; Gordon Tucker and Michael Paley, both rabbis; Gaia Smith, a potter; Jeff Bogursky, a virtual reality specialist; Judith Tumin, a middle school principal; Doni Kipnis, a fishery manager; Art Green, a professor and antique glass dealer; and Adil Lacheb, a café worker.

It's important that you love your work. Never stay with a job just because it's a job. Work at things that you love and that fill up your life.

Over the years, famous people have come in to eat at Columbus Café (the café my business partner Arthur Gordon and I own). Noam, since you eat there every day (those endless Hebrew National salami sandwiches!), you know better than anyone that Columbus Café is not a trendy place; it's more an Upper-West-Side-of-Manhattan-neighborhood kind of place, so if some famous person is eating there, it's probably because he lives nearby and got hungry. But for me, the most thrilling person who ever ate there (besides various members of my family, of course!) was Maya Angelou. I was downstairs in my office and happened to look up at the TV monitor, when I noticed someone walk in accompanied by a small entourage. My interest was piqued, and as I peered intently, I suddenly realized that the central person in the group looked a lot like Maya Angelou. I rushed upstairs, unceremoniously shoved all my workers out of the way, and was in time to act as the cashier for the transaction. After she had eaten, on her way out of the store, she made it a point to come up to me to ask me if I were the owner. "Yes," I replied, desperately hoping Big Al hadn't been rude to her when he served her. (You remember Big Al, whose notion of "the customer is always right" was to flatly refuse to prepare orders that offended his gastronomic sensibilities: "Lady, in my country, we don't eat mustard with cheese. You can have butter or mayo.") "I just wanted to let you know," she continued, "that the grilled vegetable sandwich was delicious and so huge that I couldn't finish it. But I had the rest wrapped to take home with me!" "What an amazing woman," I thought to myself, "this woman who danced with Alvin Ailey, recited poetry before presidents, and paused to acknowledge me with a word about a sandwich because she had noticed and understood that I both recognized and admired her."

Nobility and poverty are not synonymous terms. People who confuse the two are often immature or obsessed with money.

In each of your relationships, know how you need to be nurtured, and make sure you are receiving that essential nurturing. I take it for granted, knowing each of you as I do, that you yourselves will give generously. But it is also important to know how to receive as well, and to understand what it is that you need to receive.

Most people in life are not born with the skill of knowing how to manage their time. It is a skill people have to learn, and I consider it to be one of the single most important life skills I've had to master.

Don't waste your time. By this, I don't mean "overprogram your life," which is often what people who want to be successful or productive think this means. I myself tend to fall into the trap of being too efficient at time management and I often accomplish more in a day than is good for me. So *don't* maximize every minute of your day. But *do* use your time productively and efficiently, keeping time free for unexpected things. Time is a gift and is precious. I learned this when my mother died at the age of fifty-three and I realized how many things she had yet intended to do with her life.

When you buy a new dining room table, either buy the custom-made protective felt table pads or, if they are too expensive, get the padded table liner as a protector. Even with the protector, always use hot pads before you place anything hot on a wooden table. In other words (Noam!), take care of your stuff!

Art Green taught a Hasidic parable about a father and son traveling along a road together. When the son decided not to continue farther until he had picked berries, the father continued on his journey alone. The father cautioned the son to call out every few minutes to the father and the father would answer him; for as long as the son could hear the father's voice, he would know the father was nearby. But, continued the father, "as soon as you can no longer hear my answer, know that you are lost, and run with all your strength to find me." This is, of course, a parable about God and people, but I believe it is also true about relationships. In a relationship you care deeply about, never let the other stray too far away, because when you finally notice that she has moved away, it may be too late to call her back to you.

When you are in a relationship, pay attention to small things. One of the scariest things I know to be true is that most marriages don't break up over any large dramatic event. Most marriages are so delicately balanced that a very small decision or neglect or misunderstanding can permanently disable the entire mechanism.

Hang your sports jackets on wooden hangers. Wire hangers ruin the shape of clothes.

Process anger. Don't mask it with humor or bury it away somewhere. Anger, real anger, is like yeast. It can become its own living organism and bubble away, spreading everywhere. So *learn to talk*.

Noam, there was a pretty terrible rite of passage that all twelve-to fourteen-year-old boys in Manhattan (including you) went through when you were growing up. During those two years, you were mugged on the way home from school by older kids on a half-dozen different occasions. I was the agonized witness to your helplessness and quiescent rage, and, although suffused with pity, I had no way to comfort you. When you finally hit upon the notion of taking up weight lifting and bodybuilding, I realized immediately how brilliantly you had solved your problem. You were able to conquer your own feelings of help-lessness, and, coincidentally, after the first six months, no one ever mugged you again.

I began to exercise regularly at the age of forty-three and took up tennis at the age of forty-six. It's important all your life to conceive of yourself as someone continuing to grow.

When you walk along the street, look into people's faces as you pass them. Kayla, you taught me this when you began your own personal homelessness project as a student at the Prozdor Hebrew High School program. You would use your allowance to buy food and drinks, which you distributed to the homeless on your walk up to school at 122nd Street. I didn't know you were doing this until a month into your project, when I joined you one day on your walk. You greeted all the homeless people by name whether or not they needed food. I was awed, as I have often been, by the purity of your soul, and you taught me to extend my rule about looking at people as I pass them on the street even to those who, in our society, have no faces.

Noam, when you transferred to Trevor Day School, I wanted you to continue your Jewish education and convinced you to try the Prozdor Hebrew High School program that Kayla was finding so meaningful. You tried it, and to my surprise, continued for two years. After you quit, I asked you why you had continued to go for as long as you did and you replied, "I liked hanging out with the kids during the bagel breaks between classes." Even in the ninth grade, you had the most finely honed social skills of any human being I've ever met (with the possible exception of Cousin Richard)!

When you buy a car that has a "donut" instead of a full-size spare tire, try to replace the donut with a real tire. Otherwise, you make double work for yourself when you have a flat.

Never, ever buy jewelry or art as an investment. Buy it only if you like it enough to wear it or look at it.

Noam, you are the worst packer in the whole world! You never forget to pack your zip drive or the Nintendo 64; but underwear and socks evidently fit into your category of nonessentials. So this piece of advice is specifically for you: When you're packing for a trip and are tight for space, stuff your socks and underwear into your shoes (you do seem to remember to pack shoes, so if you get into the habit of stuffing underwear and socks in, at least you know you'll have them). Also, pack liquids, like shampoo, in Ziploc bags, so they don't spill all over your green suitcase like they did on the way back from London three years ago!

I have been enormously impressed over the years watching each of you choose friends. You each have high-quality people in your lives whom you love and who, I know, will be your friends for as long as you live. For you, Kayla, I'm talking about Liz, and for you, Noam, who else but Emil? My friend Ann Appelbaum has always been just such an extraordinary friend to me. She has very high standards, and I have always been careful to meet her standards. This is because I know Ann to be someone who will be my lifelong friend, and when I admit someone to this category of friendship, I am acknowledging that the presence of this person in my life is critical to my own well-being and happiness, just as I am critical to hers. Always be careful to nurture such relationships, because they are a gift.

Noam, language is very important. You especially need to learn to talk through what you are feeling. If you force yourself to articulate your experience, that articulation will become a life-long habit.

Be balanced in all you do. But remember that it is sometimes worthwhile to feel and act passionately.

I am not a believer in relative morality. Lots of things in life are really simple and clear and there's no good to be served in pretending there are grays. An example of this is Woody Allen having an affair with the daughter of his lover.

Avoid fried foods whenever possible.

If you don't know what you are talking about, shut up. This may seem self-evident, but you would not believe how many people talk authoritatively about things they don't really know. And don't assume that everyone who speaks with self-assurance knows what he is talking about. Some people manage to figure out the self-assurance part without figuring out the actual content part.

If a glass is chipped, throw it out.

Before Rosh Hashanah, Ann Appelbaum and I frequently coordinate our menus so that we can then swap those foods that the other family loves (Neal loves my meatballs and Kayla loves Ann's broccoli soufflé). Ann also frequently makes her mother Teedy's salmon en croûte recipe, which I love and which is not hard to make. Buy frozen puff pastry dough and defrost 2 sheets. Then poach or bake 3 to 4 pounds of salmon until mostly done (or use leftover or canned salmon). When the salmon is cool, remove all the bones and break the fish up into small pieces. Add a grated large onion (Vidalia is nice, but any onion will do), a bunch of dill, washed and chopped, salt, pepper, a cup of low-fat sour cream, and bread crumbs to hold it all together (let's say ½ to 1 cup). Then arrange half the salmon mixture down the center of one sheet of the dough and bring the dough sides up so they meet in the middle. Pinch all the ends closed and transfer with the seam side down to an ungreased cookie sheet. Fill the second sheet with the remaining salmon mixture. Beat an egg and brush the top of the pastry with the beaten egg and then sprinkle on sesame seeds. Bake at 350 degrees until brown. This freezes really well. Just make sure not to overbrown it so that it can be reheated once you defrost it.

Drink water and eat fresh fruits and vegetables.

When people are trying to sell you something, they often try to make the problems associated with whatever they are trying to sell seem trivial or easily surmountable. Try to make slow decisions in such cases. Keep in mind that the schmuck who's going to get stuck ironing out all the problems with whatever it is you've bought is you.

Unless there's a reason not to, always build on the highest point of a piece of land.

In the war between biting wit and kindness, as much as I enjoy quick repartee, there is also something to be said for letting kindness win. I failed this rule the year you, Kayla, came home from college for Rosh Hashanah sporting purple hair. The purple hair itself was bad enough, but what I found particularly galling was the fact that we in the family were all going to have to smilingly support your right to look hideous in front of 1,800 members of your father's synagogue. Sure enough, you were the talk of the congregation that New Year, and I endured the comments and stares with smiling unconcern until one particularly obnoxious seventy-four-year-old bleached-blond woman cornered me and asked with spurious sympathy, "Whatever could have possessed Kayla to do something as outrageous as this?" "I would imagine," I replied tartly, "that what possessed Kayla is the same thing that possesses you when you choose to dye your hair blond." I am not proud of that remark.

In life, it's important to know when to give up. I failed every science course I ever took. Finally, it came time for me to graduate from college and I knew I would not be able to meet the science requirement. I petitioned U. Mass. to be exempted from the requirement, explaining that I had never been able to pass a science course. The committee met, agreed that my science record was abysmal, and exempted me from the requirement.

One would think my science record would have taught me something when it came to dealing with my children and schools. Unfortunately, it didn't, until it was almost too late. Noam, I didn't do well by you when you had difficulties in school. You were attending the same school that Kayla had attended, and while it was the perfect school for Kayla and gave her an extraordinary intellectual foundation, for you, with your vastly different learning style, it was the wrong school and you were quietly miserable. I was reluctant to switch schools, reasoning that you were already into the sixth grade and if you could make it through to the eighth grade, you could graduate with your class. I have to thank one of your teachers (who did not last at the school—for all the right reasons) that year for inadvertently helping me to make the right decision.

At a parent–teacher conference, you waited apprehensively in the hallway outside your classroom while we met with that teacher. To clarify a point that we had raised, she called you into the room. She had a smile affixed to her face, but she addressed you with an air of exaggerated patience that arrested my attention and made me suddenly realize the amount of misery you were enduring each day of your life in her classroom. She was not able to meet your particular learning needs and I saw clearly what I should have understood before: there was no reason to assume that the school that worked for one of my children would necessarily be the right choice for my other children. The next morning, I let you know that you and I would begin the process of finding a new school for the following year. Thank God we found our way to Trevor Day School, where you received the amount of support accompanied with clearly defined expectations that you needed in order to function academically. I remain enormously grateful to Trevor, years later, because they took you in and helped you grow into self-assurance.

Kayla, I had a different problem with you. Your first school nurtured you and helped you flower and grow intellectually, so that you had the pick of any of the best private schools in New York for high school. Along with Dalton and Friends Seminary, you had been admitted to the top public school in the city—Stuyvesant. You went to visit Friends (your first choice) and loved the warm, nurturing, thoroughly intellectual atmosphere there. You also went to visit Stuyvesant, where you were intimidated by the vast numbers of students surging through the halls and frightened by the competitive rigor of the exchanges between students and teachers. You let us know your first choice was Friends, where you instinctively knew your intellectual interests would be nurtured and supported. I had a different agenda for you. I was concerned that you begin to develop the skills to make your way in a less nurturing environment than you were likely to encounter at Friends. I encouraged you to try Stuyvesant for a year, but you got that mulish set to your mouth as we discussed it. Finally, I hit upon the notion of offering you a trip to Paris if you would try Stuyvesant for just one year. Paris did the trick and you agreed with alacrity. We had a fabulous trip which both of us remember with pleasure. (I'll never forget the moment you turned to me on the airplane ride over to ask me if we absolutely had to be mother and daughter during the trip. Puzzled, I asked you what alternative you had in mind and you replied, "Couldn't we just be friends?" I was charmed by your request and acquiesced, and we then shared the loveliest two weeks together.) You attended Stuyvesant that freshman year and were miserable. I realized I had made a big mistake in hoping that you would be able to figure out the skills to negotiate a school of more than 3,000 students. I waited all year for your request to transfer to Friends, perfectly prepared to stick to my part of the bargain that you could transfer after that year. You stuck it out, however, and suddenly, at the start of tenth grade, moved forward aggressively to carve out the high school experience you wanted for yourself. As you later explained it to me, "Eema, I spent the first year at Stuyvesant waiting for one of the teachers to come up to me, as they would have at Heschel, to put her arm around my shoulders and tell me that I am a wonderful writer and would I like to write for the creative writing magazine? Then I suddenly realized in June that year that if what I was really saying was that I wanted to write for the school magazine, why couldn't I move forward myself to make that happen?" I was careful not to look too exultant when you reported that story to me, but it took a lot of self-restraint not to whoop in joy at the magnificent leap into maturity that you had made.

Many problems grow if they are not addressed when they arise. This was true for a couple I once knew. When they renovated their home twenty-five years ago, they neglected to get a new Certificate of Occupancy even though they knew they needed one. Now, twenty-five years later, they would like to sell their home but know that it is unsalable without a C of O. In the intervening years, the laws have become more stringent and their twenty-five-year-old renovation will no longer pass building codes.

If an offer seems too good to be true, it often is. Use your common sense.

If an offer seems too good to be true, it still pays to investigate it. I was once reading the *Shopper's Guide* newspaper in the Berkshires. Someone had put an ad in the paper that read "Free in-ground pool. Take it away." I read the ad aloud to a visitor, who said, "Don't call. It's just a come-on from a pool company." I was, nonetheless, intrigued by the ad and decided to call. The ad had been placed by an elderly man who had a metal-sided in-ground pool that he no longer used. He was willing to give away the pool, since he wanted to plant an arbor in its place. I called an excavator immediately to find out how much it would cost to dig out the pool and install it at our house. The excavator explained that we would also have to buy a pool liner, since the sides can be reused on a pool, but the liner cannot. I spent the next hour getting information on the price of a new liner and by the next day, everything was arranged and the excavator had begun the work of digging out the pool and reinstalling it at our house. That's the story of how we got the pool all of you loved so much in Great Barrington.

I have often found that if you behave with a generosity of spirit, people will respond to you the same way. But this is not always true.

Don't clutter up your mind with junk. If it's really and continuously difficult for you to grasp something, find someone else to do it for whom it is not difficult. I have often traded real estate advice, which for me is easy, for help programming the VCR, which everyone knows is *really hard*.

Try to take stock of yourself and where you are going every few months. That way, if you are heading off course, you can get yourself straightened out before you end up too far adrift.

Get in touch with the still small voice inside you. That voice is steady and clear and you can trust it and use it as your guide all your life.

And know before
whom you will
one day stand in
judgement . . .

**E**very day of his life, my grandfather would say, *"Baruch Hashem Yom Yom!"* (literally, "Bless God for each day!").

When I was a teenager, I began reading serious philosophical works. I concluded that God did not rule the world, that in fact we and God were partners. One Yom Kippur, in consonance with my new thinking, I decided not to "fall *korim*" (prostrate myself) for the *aleinu* prayer. My zaydee, who had eagle eyes, even for the upstairs women's balcony, asked me to take a walk with him during the break in services. He wondered, he told me, why I hadn't fallen *korim*. I explained that it was a *"neue velt"* (literally, a "new world") now and the old-fashioned ideas of God ruling everything and people scurrying around to do God's command no longer made sense. Zaydee listened and then asked thoughtfully, "Sherelleh, tell me more about this *neue velt*." I did, telling him all about the things I had been reading and thinking. When I finished, my grandfather said to me, "This new world you speak about I understand. But there is one thing I do not understand. In this new world, before whom will you bow?"

After my mother died, I wanted to have another baby to name after her. In Jewish families, this notion of naming is very important. It is a way of continuing the life and the soul of the person who has died, of passing on his legacy to the next generation. So after her death, I tried for six long, heartbreaking years to get and stay pregnant (I kept miscarrying—for no apparent reason). Finally, the miscarriages having sapped my eagerness and dignity, I decided that I should rejoice in the gift of the two healthy children I already had and not try to conceive anymore. The very next morning after I came to that decision, I woke up nauseous, threw up, and woke up your father to tell him that I was pregnant again. I resigned myself to more heartbreak. About a month later, I had a dream in which God revealed to me that the pregnancy would be fine and the baby was a boy. I woke up from the dream at 3:00 A.M. "Holy smokes!" I thought wildly. "It's a boy!" Somehow, it had never occurred to me that this baby, who was supposed to be named Ruth, after my mother, could possibly be a boy (to this day, I am astounded at my own hubris in this, but so it was). I realized immediately that God had sent me the dream so that I could relax and enjoy the pregnancy and so that I could get used to the idea of having another boy, which, believe me, took a lot of getting used to (I actually toyed with the idea, mercifully brief, of naming him Ruth). Three months into the pregnancy, my obstetrician, during a routine visit, said, "I'll be scheduling the amniocentesis in the next two weeks." "Oh, that won't be necessary," I replied brightly. "This baby is fine. There won't be any problems with this pregnancy." "Really?" asked the obstetrician in some amusement. "How do you know that?" "I had a dream," I explained. "A dream?" she asked with patent skepticism. "Yes," I explained patiently. "Sometimes, though not very often, the women in my family dream. The dreams are messages from God and they are always true." The doctor eyed me for a long moment and then, having apparently decided to forgo the psychiatric referral, shrugged and responded firmly, "Nevertheless, you'll need to have an amnio at your age." There ensued a lively debate, since I felt strongly that with the information I had, the amnio was an unnecessary procedure, but finally I gave in. The day of the amnio arrived and the technician performing the amnio asked me, in preparation for the event, whether I wanted to know the sex of the child. "I already know the sex of the child," I responded warily, certain she too would think me crazy. "It's a boy and he's healthy." "Really?" inquired the technician. "How do you know that?" "Message from God," I responded succinctly. "Sure you want to bother with the amnio, then?" she inquired politely.

Before you move into a new home, it is our family custom (other families have different customs) to bring in salt, bread, and candles. The bread is brought as a sign that there should always be food in the house, the candles, so that there should always be light (celebration, etc.), and the salt, so that we never forget our tears at the loss of the Temple in Jerusalem.

Once I was selling an apartment building I owned in Manhattan. There were a number of interested buyers and after long, detailed negotiations, I arrived at a price of $1,900,000 with the buyer who seemed to me the most serious. After we agreed on the price, the buyer asked for three days to "think about" the deal. I was angry, since I believe the time to "think about" a deal is before one enters negotiations. Nonetheless, I told the buyer that he could certainly take three days or three weeks to think about the deal, but that I would not consider the price binding until the contract was signed. The buyer said he was willing to take the risk and we agreed to speak again in three days. When we spoke later that week, he told me he wanted to proceed with the deal. I replied that in the interim another offer had emerged and that he would have to pay $1,950,000 in order to buy the building. He was clearly nonplussed but said he would call back in an hour. An hour later, he called back and said he would pay the new price but wanted to go to contract the next morning, which I agreed to do. On the day of the closing two months later, while the buyer sat across the table from me looking on, I wrote a check to the Jewish Communal Fund for $50,000.

Noam, you have talked about enjoying synagogue because it's a place where "everybody knows your name and they're always glad you came." For that reason, wherever you live, find a Jewish community and live within walking distance to it. This is not about being insular. It is about staying close to the family.

You should always have certain things in your home. These include a box of candles, Shabbat candlesticks, a siddur (prayer book), a Bible, a good vegetable knife, and ammonia (with which you can clean many things).

You should always hang a mezuzah on the doorpost of your home within a month after moving in. After you've hung it, don't ignore its existence. Try to notice it hanging there, since it is the mezuzah that is the outward sign that one is living in a Jewish home.

My friend Ann told me that to this day, fifteen years later, she regrets the mistake she made when she compiled the guest list for her wedding. She debated and then omitted, for reasons that now seem silly, two couples who were forever afterward hurt by their exclusion. I once made the same mistake myself and was firmly, and correctly, rebuked for my lapse in judgment. From this we learn that when planning a celebration, if you are in doubt about whether to invite someone, it's best to operate on the basis of generosity of spirit and invite him or her.

The corollary to this is: *Never* use a *simcha* as a way to retaliate against someone. Someone I knew well but who disliked a position I took at a board meeting once decided not to invite me to her son's Bar Mitzvah. I thought a long time about what to do and finally decided to send the boy a Bar Mitzvah present and a note, because I felt proud of his accomplishment and wanted to acknowledge that milestone in his life. Some weeks later, I received a note of apology from his mother. It's more than a decade later, and I have kept the note as a reminder to myself never to make the same mistake. The family rule is, when you are planning a *simcha*, try to let the feelings of joy from the celebration overflow so that the *simcha* can become a vehicle to repair and heal old pains.

Aunt Debby is a midwife and an in vitro fertility specialist at Bikur Holim Hospital in Jerusalem. One day, my friend Minna called me. Desperate to get pregnant, she was taking a specific fertility drug. "You're one of the best networkers I know," she began. "There's a shortage in America of the fertility drug I take. I'm frantic to get more, and I've called every connection I could think of in the entire country and I can't locate any anywhere! Can you think of a way to help me?" Minna's connections in the medical world were considerable, since both her parents were doctors, and I knew that if they had pulled out all the stops and been unable to locate the drug, the situation was really serious. I was eager to help Minna. Five years earlier, on her honeymoon in Jerusalem, she had conceived a baby who, nine months later, had been born and lived only a matter of hours. Burying that child had been one of the hardest things our community had been through and we had all mourned Minna and Dan's loss. On the heels of that tragedy, they had never been able to conceive again. I replied, "My sister-in-law Debby is an in vitro specialist in Jerusalem. Maybe she can get the drug and we can find someone coming back who can bring it to you." I called Debby the next morning and explained Minna's history and her current problem. "What drug is she taking?" asked Debby. I told her the name of the drug. "Does Minna know that you called me here in Jerusalem?" she asked. "Of course she does!" I replied impatiently. "Well, I can probably get her the drug," continued Debby, "but she really doesn't need it. She'll—" "Deb," I interrupted with growing annoyance, "she most certainly does need it. You can't possibly diagnose a fertility problem long distance. The only question on the table is: Can you get it for her?" "I'll call you back in a few hours," she replied, and I could tell by the tone in her voice that she had just shrugged. "Fine," I said curtly. "I'll wait for your call." Debby did indeed call me back in few hours and reported that there was a worldwide shortage of the drug but that she had managed to locate a month's supply in Eilat and was having it brought to Jerusalem that week. We worked out a plan for my friend Anita, who was then visiting Jerusalem, to get it back to New York and I called Minna with the good news. She was beside herself with joy and I told her the medicine would be in New York within two weeks. Sure enough, two weeks later, Anita arrived on my doorstep with the medicine and I called Minna with the news that it had arrived. She replied that she'd be over later to pick it up. She did not come that day, nor the next, nor the next. Finally, after a week had passed, I called Minna and angrily reminded her that we had all gone to considerable effort, not to mention expense, to procure this emergency medicine for her and she could bloody well make the time to come by to pick it up. She came by within the hour and shamefacedly shared her secret. I called Debby as soon as Minna had left my house and I exclaimed in excitement, "Deb, you'll never believe what happened to Minna!" "Sure I will," she interrupted me, laughing. "She's pregnant!" I stopped dead. "Okay, who told you?" I queried in laughing resignation. "No one told me," she responded. "I tried to tell *you* the day you called that Minna wasn't going to need the fertility drug. I've been doing fertility for more than a decade. I figured that if she conceived so easily the first time, in her case the odds were that there was probably nothing biologically wrong. She just needed to establish an emotional link between her first child and her second. Remember," she continued, "that her first child was conceived in Jerusalem. So I thought it probable that what Minna really needed to conceive this time was to be told that the fertility drug from Jerusalem was coming. I wasn't sure, but I thought it a good possibility that she never actually needed to have or take the drug!" "You're amazing!" I gasped. "Not me," she replied, "God's mysterious ways!"

My friends Everett and Mary Gendler bought land in Great Barrington, Massachusetts, two years before I bought our first house there. They camped on their 170 beautiful acres every summer for eighteen years, caretaking the land, weeding and tending the stream, and living lives that have been a model for me in their commitment to simplicity, frugality, and acknowledgment of the beauty of God's world. After eighteen years of camping, they finally decided, in their retirement, to build a house on their land. Their neighbor heard through the grapevine about their plans to build and faxed them an offer of $700,000 for their land, offering an all-cash deal and the ability to close immediately. They reported this to me the week after they had received the offer, when I visited them at the site. "Oh, my God!" I squealed. "A home run! When do you close?" "Close?" asked Everett in puzzlement. "Close what?" he asked, obviously bewildered by the turn the conversation had taken. "The sale!" I answered impatiently. "When will the sale go through?" "We're not selling our land!" answered Mary indignantly. "What do you mean you're not selling the land? Did you counteroffer?" Now I was the one bewildered. "Of course we didn't counteroffer," responded Everett gently. "The land is not for sale." "Of course it's for sale," I answered. "The guy just hasn't offered you the right price yet." "No," said Everett. "There is no right price. We have been caretaking this land for eighteen years, getting acquainted with it so we would be prepared to build on it with respect and love. That's what we plan to do." "Besides which," added Mary, "our neighbor is wealthy enough to think that everything is for sale; it's good for people who believe this to learn that not everything has a price!" "But the way to teach him a lesson is to make him overpay for your land!" I wailed, dumbfounded, and they laughed at my response. In my heart, I know they are right because of who they are. And I do want to learn their ways because I think their ways are good ways. But part of me is still the businesswoman who can't believe they didn't counteroffer at $1,300,000 and then get a Realtor to take them out to look at other beautiful 170-acre parcels.

In your lives, try to become who *you* need yourself to be, not who you think other people need you to be. My friend Arthur, who is often gruffly solicitous of my welfare, urged me to try to appear gentler than I am or risk intimidating people I encounter. I considered his advice, and then realized that I was too old to learn the knack of subterfuge. This intransigence to hiding has become a more powerful part of me as the years have passed, even though I still believe that it is good for me to try to change those parts of myself I don't love. But I know that the parts of me that are deeply a part of my being need to stay close to me. One of my favorite Hasidic tales is the one about Reb Zusya. The story is told that when Reb Zusya was close to death, he called his students together to teach them one last thing. "I do not worry," he taught, "that when I die I will be called to account before the Holy One and asked why I could not have been more like Moses. What I worry about," Reb Zusya continued, "is that when I die, I will be called to account before the Holy One and asked why I could not have been more like Zusya."

Another of my favorite Hasidic stories is the one about Rabbi Noah, who succeeded his father, Rabbi Mordechai, after Rabbi Mordechai's death. His disciples noted that there were a number of ways that Rabbi Noah conducted himself differently from his father. The disciples talked among themselves about this and then raised the issue directly with Rabbi Noah. Replied Rabbi Noah, "I do exactly as my father did. My father did not imitate and I do not imitate."

Some years ago, you may recall that for almost two months I was away from home most of the week and came home only on weekends. That was when my father collapsed quite suddenly in Florida and was brought to a medical center where his condition remained undiagnosed for long enough so that sepsis developed from his diseased gallbladder. Aunt Miriam (my father's second wife—he married my mother's younger sister after my mother died, and that's another story) called me hysterically crying three nights after his collapse because she realized he was dying, and she could not get the hospital to become aggressive about either diagnosing or treating him. After I calmed her down, I got on the phone to the hospital administrator and informed her that my husband was a partner in a New York law firm (you know perfectly well he was not) and that they had better wake up the nearest specialist and get him in to see my father within the next hour, or there would be hell to pay by morning. I also informed her that I myself would be out on the first plane in the morning and in the meantime, I would call back in an hour to find out what the specialist had to say. I spent the next hour booking myself on a flight, packing a suitcase, and crying. When I called back the hospital, I was informed that my father had slipped into a coma and was being transferred to intensive care, where they would begin to run tests to determine his medical condition (imagine having a patient in the hospital for three days without performing one medical test to determine his medical condition!). By 11:00 the next morning, I was in the hospital and began the task of gleaning information and following the various diagnoses and then determining who were the best specialists for the medical problems as they surfaced. Despite the best medical care available, his condition worsened as his kidney and lungs began to fail. He was placed on a respirator, which, after a while, did most of the breathing for him. This situation went on for more than two weeks, and finally, the hospital administrator came to see me in the intensive care unit to tell me that there had been a high-level meeting of the hospital management and that they felt the time had arrived for me to consider turning off the respirator. I had buried the mother I was not finished with ten years earlier, and I had no intention of burying the father I had only begun to really know after my mother died. I told the administrator that I had nursed my father through numerous illnesses (which was true) and I would know if he were dead. And I knew as certainly as I had ever known anything in my life that my father was alive. The administrator tried to pressure me and then gave up, promising to return to continue to "talk about it." My bold assertion notwithstanding, I was frightened enough by her visit to corner the lung specialist who, by now, was managing the case, and ask him to tell me when the time came that he thought the case was hopeless. I explained that I wanted my brother in Israel to be able to see my father before, God forbid, he died and the journey would take two days to complete (Jerusalem–Tel Aviv–New York–Miami–Boca Raton). The doctor said he would, of course, tell me. I called Mark in Israel to let him know these latest developments. We had been speaking two or three times each day and Mark was following closely all the medical developments, and trying to make the best judgment he could on when to come to Florida (I had been discouraging him from making the trip, since I wanted Dad to be out of the coma and able to see Mark when he arrived). We agreed that Mark would still hold off coming. In the meantime, I continued to do all the things I could think of to help my father. I talked to him; I sang to him; I played his favorite Nat King Cole music (which the man in the next bed greatly enjoyed); I stroked his hand; I urged him to come back to us. Finally, two days later, the lung specialist said Dad had taken a turn for the worse and I should call my brother in Israel if I wanted him here before the end. I called Mark and told him what the doctor had said. Mark said he would get on the next plane and then quietly asked me if I thought Dad was dying. I answered as honestly as I could that I still believed Dad might recover but that I myself was finally frightened to death and needed my brother to handle this with me. Mark arrived two days later at the airport in Miami and I drove there to pick him up. On the way in from the airport, Mark asked me to stop at the nearest bookstore. At this, I exploded in horror. "I know you're a book lover who can't find many English-language books in Israel, but this does *not* seem to me to be an opportune time to go book shopping!" Mark grinned engagingly at me and said, "Never mind. Humor me and stop." Which, of course, I did. He rushed to the "Alternative Medicine" section of the bookstore and bought all the books on reflexology that they had there (three). We continued on to the hospital, where Mark raced to Dad's bedside. Dad was in the same condition he had been in for two weeks, but Mark was visibly shaken by seeing our father lying waxen-faced and lifeless in a coma. At the end of fifteen minutes, we left Dad's bedside and retired to the waiting room. Handing me one of the three books, Mark said, "Here. Read it fast. This is the latest thing in Israel." I was loath to explore the mysteries of reflexology but unwilling to deny my brother, who, as far as I could see, was determined to process the impending loss of our father by pursuing useless alternative medicine schemes. But read I did, and when I'd finished the first book, he threw me over the second, which he had himself just finished, and then the third. So far as I remember (I have never had occasion to use reflexology from that time to this), reflexology believes that each organ of the body has a corresponding location on the foot of a human being. If you wish to heal the lungs, you find the lung location on the foot and massage that location. Likewise for kidneys, heart, liver, etc. Reading the books served to lighten my mood and my principal reaction was "Foot massage. Okay. I can handle that." So, when we were allowed back in to see Dad, we gently folded back the covers from his feet and began (with continual referral back to the books to check their illustrations of feet) to surreptitiously massage his feet. Why surreptitiously? As I pointed out to Mark, I was perfectly prepared, if it made Mark happy and caused Dad no harm, to massage Dad's feet until my hands ached. I was not, however, prepared to explain to the vigilant and not particularly alternative-type intensive care nurses what it was I was doing to the feet of a man lying lifeless in a coma. So, after the first hour, we decided that one of us would massage the lung section of Dad's feet while the other of us kept watch for nurses, doctors, and other less enlightened types. I didn't object to the project, but there was never a question in my mind that we two were playing at some ritual whose purpose was to allow my brother to let my father die and be able to feel that he had contributed all he had to give in trying to heal him. Now here's the weird part. My father continued to linger in a coma. But two days after we began the foot massage, we arrived at the hospital at 7:30 A.M. just as the lung doctor was leaving Dad's bedside. "You know," began the lung doctor, with a puzzled expression, "I find this very strange, and I want to make a few calls to colleagues, since I've never seen anything like this, but your father seems to have made some slight progress and could be breathing on his own a bit more than he was able to yesterday." And with that, he departed. I stood rooted to the spot dumbstruck as my brother winked at me and rolled up his sleeves to begin the day's massage. Later that same morning, the kidney specialist saw us and said conversationally, "I wanted to call you to let you know that, as unlikely as it might seem, your father's one remaining kidney seems to be beginning to function somewhat, and I've ordered the discontinuation of the dialysis." As he walked away, my eyes flew to my brother, who explained with a twinkle, "I began massaging the kidney foot-spot yesterday afternoon. I figured Dad wouldn't want to be on dialysis for the rest of his life when he came out of the coma." And so it went, with each organ regenerating itself for the next two days, until Dad opened up his eyes and asked plaintively just where the hell he was and how come he was so thirsty. Mark asked me in a whisper later that jubilant day, "Do you think we should tell the doctors about the reflexology?" "Absolutely not!" I replied. "How can you possibly expect them to believe something that we both know perfectly well is ridiculous!" "Sure," said Mark with another twinkle, "be completely selfish and deny everyone else in the world the benefit of our extraordinary medical experience!" Actually, though, what I believed then is what I continue to believe now, ten years later: that, after all, it was all in God's hands, and God was content to let us have our own little joke along the way.

Sometime in your life you will probably meet a holy person. Be very careful in judging who is holy. Most of the Jewish leaders I have met, even those that the community treats as holy people, have, upon closer knowledge, not lived up to their billing. Truly holy people are few and far between. In fact, Jewish tradition tells us that there are thirty-six hidden righteous people in the world. These people do not know each other and do not know they are the righteous ones. But they are holy people and we must revere them if we suspect we have met one (I myself have met one, I know). As for the others, you must show them respect as you would to any human being, but there is no need to give them undue recognition.

I've never liked to pray in a synagogue with too much decorum. I find that the silence disturbs my ability to pray. I need the background sounds of children chortling behind me to verify that I'm praying in a real community.

My friend Leah told me she went to a psychiatric conference and met a man she hadn't seen in twenty years. He delivered a paper in which he talked about his son who, eighteen years earlier, with 1500 on his college board scores and a brilliant high school academic record, had been granted early admission to Harvard. Instead of attending Harvard, however, the boy had a breakdown and was diagnosed with schizophrenia. That boy, eighteen years later, was now a man of thirty-six, finally responding to new medication, and graduating from a local community college. Leah told me this when I had just finished complaining about Noam's forgetting yet another orthodontist appointment (which endeared him no end to Dr. Kossowan, I know). I felt ashamed of my complaints and grateful to Leah for her gently administered rebuke.

Once your father became a rabbi, I learned more about the inner lives of people in the congregation than I had known before. One of the things I learned is that more people walk around with broken hearts than you could possibly believe.

My friend, whose daughter had a nervous breakdown in college, owns a family business. While the daughter was recovering from her breakdown, she asked her father to hire her to work in his business. He was about to refuse, since his business requires constant contact with clients and he was nervous about the risk of employing his daughter. He consulted with a friend, who advised him with the following words: "If you have a family business and there is no place in that business for your daughter when she needs such a place, then there is no place for your daughter anywhere else in the world."

My friend Anita bought Barson's Hardware Store in Manhattan from her father, Barney, before he died and she now runs the store with her husband, David. Seven years after Barney's death, Anita still has some of the white shirts that her father wore to work at Barson's. When she is feeling low, she wears one of those shirts and says on those days she is taking Barney to work with her.

Noam, you've become very conscious of your appearance. In a family where no one seems to pay much attention to what they are wearing or what they look like (can we ever forget Kayla's crew-cut-bordering-on-baldness phase?), I kept waiting for you to outgrow this as you got older. That doesn't seem to be happening. Instead, you have taught yourself how to iron and are now assiduous about ironing all your clothes before you wear them. I find this puzzling and yet oddly endearing. The only tip I have to offer you on this subject is that when you dry permanent press shirts, if you take them out of the dryer and put them on hangers when they are nearly dry rather than fully dry, they will wrinkle less.

You probably already know this from my acidic comments whenever I've lent our vacation home to friends. In case, however, my comments were not clear enough (or in case you think they did not apply to you), I want to reiterate that good breeding requires you to wash out the bathtub and the sink when you are an overnight guest in someone's house. You would not believe how many people do not observe this simple courtesy. Also, if you borrow someone's home, you should arrange and pay for a cleaning service to come in at the end of your stay. If this is beyond your budget, plan to scrub the kitchen and baths as well as dust and vacuum on your last day there.

When I was growing up, everybody's energy seemed to be directed to earning a living, and there was never time or money or leisure to notice the details of life. I myself, therefore, used to be terrible at noting details, and it took Chaim Potok to break me of this. The first book I ever cowrote and coedited was called *The First Jewish Catalog*. I was twenty-three years old when that book was published and it was an immediate, phenomenal, and quite unanticipated success. My editor on that book was Chaim Potok, the well-known writer (before he quit his day job, he was the editor in chief of the Jewish Publication Society). Chaim unwittingly trained me to see things I had never noticed before. Here's how he did it. After we submitted the manuscript to him, he called us to tell us that we needed to do some editing but that he would accept the manuscript for publication. Chaim then asked us to meet with him about the book. He opened the meeting by remarking, "The manuscript you've submitted has a very contemporary and fresh feel to it. What thoughts do you have on the design of the book?" I sat there mute as he stared at us with those piercing dark eyes waiting for an answer to a question he clearly thought had an answer. Finally, when the silence had lengthened beyond the ability of my nerves to survive, I ventured to say, "What exactly are you talking about?" He was clearly puzzled by my response. "I'm asking you what you think your book looks like," he answered with as much patience as he could muster. The subject had never before crossed my mind and I stared back at him with incomprehension. "Look," he said impatiently, handing me four different books. "Open each of these books and touch the paper. What does the difference in paper suggest to you?" A faint glimmer began to appear in my mind as I touched the different papers in each of the books. "Now," he pursued, "look at the typeface in each book and think about that." I did as he suggested. "Next," he said, "notice what the book looks like, which, incidentally, is called the design of the book, and figure out how the design gives you a sense of what the book will be like. Do you understand what I am saying?" he asked. I nodded vigorously. Light had finally dawned over marble-head. "So now, what are your thoughts about the design of your book?" None of us were prepared to answer him at that point, but I still remember what it felt like to hold a book in my hands and notice the paper for the first time.

My academic career was short-lived and unremarkable. I, however, have been (thank God) extremely successful in my work and so I've never put much stock in how well someone did academically as a measure of success. Similarly, I don't much care whether someone graduated from Harvard or from Podunk U. when I'm hiring. All I care about is how smart he is and how much of a fire burns in his belly.

Dr. Laskin told me this about her father, who ran an office in Massachusetts. When he had an important job that needed to be completed quickly, he would go out to the office floor and determine who was the busiest person there. Then he would summon that person and, in addition to that person's other work, assign him the new job. His theory was that people who work hard are used to accomplishing a lot and so, if you want something done, better to assign it to someone who works at maximum capacity. I have found this to be entirely correct and also a bit puzzling. People who are always complaining about being overworked are often unproductive, while people who accomplish a lot can always squeeze another thing in.

This is one of my *worst* traits, so I can tell you unqualifiedly that it's a bad thing: try not to judge others. My friend Anita told me about a man from her town whom she and most of the town had stopped speaking to twenty-one years earlier. The man's wife became pregnant and in response to the news, the man moved out, divorced his wife, left her alone during the pregnancy and birth, and, as a final requiem, refused to give financial support or even acknowledge his own son's existence. As of the time the son turned twenty-one years old (which was when Anita told me the story), the man had never even met his own son. That summer, Anita was at a party to which the man had been invited. She avoided him but then noticed her old friends who had moved away from town long ago talking to the man. When she had the opportunity, Anita queried her old friends on why they had maintained a relationship with the man. "It's so long ago, I suppose we can tell the story now," replied the wife. "He came home early one day and caught his ex-wife in bed with another man. His ex-wife confessed that the child she was carrying was not his child, and he left her that same night. He never wanted the story told, perhaps as a way of shielding the child. But it's so long ago, I don't suppose anyone remembers the story anyway." Human nature being what it is, everyone, of course, remembered the story quite well and I have often thought since then about how easy it is to misjudge what appears to be the clearest of tales.

When Mark married Debby, the family was horror-struck to discover that she was a vegetarian (which Mark had carefully concealed from us until *after* they were married). Keep in mind that my zaydee was a butcher, and that often, after school, when all the other kids in America were snacking on milk and cookies, the kids in our family would go to Zaydee's house and have a huge plateful of brisket and potatoes. My friend Bill Novak loves to tell the story of my first encounter with vegetarianism. When I found out, after I had invited my brother and his bride to dinner, that Debby was a vegetarian, I called Bill frantically and asked him what vegetarians eat. "You must know," he replied patiently. "They eat pasta, rice, beans, or vegetables." "You mean *side dishes*?!" I blurted out in disbelief. One of the twenty recipes I made for that first dinner (I thought I could mask the lack of brisket by serving many different dishes) was stuffed mushrooms, which became Noam's favorite and a Thanksgiving staple. The recipe is really simple. Buy a lot of large fresh mushrooms. Wipe them with a damp paper towel to clean them and separate the caps from the stems (save the stems for mushroom-barley soup). Sauté a lot of chopped onions and a few cloves of garlic (the garlic is optional—not the onions) slowly until translucent but, preferably, not brown. Put the onions in a bowl and add a few cups of bread crumbs. Squish up the mixture with some melted butter or olive oil and then add salt, pepper, and either some chicken stock or some pareve chicken bouillon mixed with water. Fill up each mushroom cap and put it in a shallow baking pan. Drizzle with melted butter or olive oil and bake at 350 degrees until done (20 minutes or so).

One of my favorite teachers at Stern College was Dr. Shelley Koenigsberg, who taught education. Dr. Koenigsberg taught me two important things. On the first day of my first education class with her, Dr. Koenigsberg passed out a twenty-page syllabus for the course. I stared in mute horror at the huge collection of books and articles we were expected to read within the three months of the course. I began gamely enough those first two weeks, spending as much as five hours a day on readings for that one course. No matter how I tried to allocate my time, however, it became increasingly clear to me that I would never be able to complete the readings for the course (indeed, in two weeks, I had not even been able to finish the first page of the syllabus!). Defeated, I scheduled an appointment with Dr. Koenigsberg and, at that meeting, explained to her how much I was enjoying the course but how convinced I was that I would never be able to complete even a quarter of the readings that she had assigned. She replied with an engaging smile, "My dear, it is best to learn early on that life is a smorgasbord from which we make choices." With that, she began to put together her papers as a signal that the meeting was over. Alarmed, I hastily tried to forestall her by asking, "What do you mean? I don't understand. Are you saying I don't have to do all the reading?" She smiled again as she finished putting away her papers. "Certainly that is something you will have to decide for yourself, isn't it?" During the ensuing weeks, I must have turned over the incident in my mind a thousand times without ever deciding what it was she meant. As the course wore on, however, knowing that I couldn't possibly complete the syllabus, but feeling like I had to do some work for the course, I found myself choosing to read selections from the syllabus based on what I found most interesting in the class lectures. Sometimes I am so incredibly thickheaded that I amaze even myself! It wasn't until the day before the final exam that I realized that I had, inadvertently, done a lot of work for the course on exactly those areas in education that interested me the most. Bingo! The smorgasbord! Dr. Koenigsberg taught me to take responsibility for my own learning, something I had never before understood was possible.

The other important thing Dr. Koenigsberg taught me is this. Twenty years later, I received a solicitation from a charity that

I had supported over the years. Glancing idly at the letter, I noticed that Dr. Koenigsberg's name was listed as a member of the board of directors. I wrote a check to the organization and added the following note: "I notice that someone named Dr. Koenigsberg is listed as a board member of your organization. If this is the same Dr. Koenigsberg who was my teacher at Stern College, please let her know that I have increased my donation this year in her honor, since she was the finest teacher I ever had." Two weeks later, I received a note from Dr. Koenigsberg acknowledging my donation and inviting me to come to visit her. When I arrived at her apartment, she opened the door, looking frailer and smaller than I remembered her. She did not remember me but was very grateful to me for remembering her class as such an important experience. When she went into the kitchen to get tea, her husband, who had joined us midway through the visit, whispered that she was dying of cancer, and that my note about her teaching could not possibly have come at a better time. I visited her on a number of occasions before she died, and she opened up after a while and told me her story. I understood then that she was dying not of cancer but of a broken heart. Teaching and education had been her whole life and she had devoted herself tirelessly to her profession (I myself could certainly remember that as true). During a serious financial crisis some years earlier, Stern College had decided to fire tenured faculty as a cost-cutting measure. Dr. Koenigsberg had been among the staff to be fired. She was not able to find another job, and although she and the other staff filed a lawsuit, the suit was not upheld and she was never able to teach again. I don't know if you can understand what it means for someone to be denied access to the one thing they love doing. She developed cancer and was dying from that cancer when my note arrived. You can imagine, I am sure, how much my note meant to her at that moment in her life. She died within three months of my reconnecting with her. I learned then how important it is to acknowledge other people whenever we have the opportunity to do so.

I've talked about how important it is to find work you love. It's even more important to find a person to love.

I knew one other person who died of a broken heart. That person was my father's best friend, Uncle Moishe. Uncle Moishe had a very pure soul and was a cantor. He had a beautiful voice and a tremendous amount of *kavannah* (spiritual focus) when he davened. He used to lead a congregation in Massachusetts, but when a High Holiday pulpit became available in his own town of Providence, Rhode Island, he became the cantor there. He led services for many years, but there arose some disgruntlement because he did not always end High Holiday services on time. The congregation sent a delegation late one summer to speak to Uncle Moishe to tell him that, despite his devotion to prayer, he would not be rehired if he did not speed up the prayers or cut something out to shorten the time. He responded that he davened according to the requirements of Jewish law and the dictates of his responsibility to the congregation. A short time later, he heard that the congregation was interviewing other candidates for the High Holiday pulpit. Heartbroken and angry, Uncle Moishe stopped speaking to the leaders of the congregation, whom he had known for most of his life. As the High Holidays grew closer, however, Uncle Moishe, who knew full well that Jewish law required him to put his emotional affairs in order for the High Holidays, called each member of the leadership to apologize for his anger. Rosh Hashanah that year began on a Sunday night. Uncle Moishe died on the Friday before Rosh Hashanah, and was buried on Sunday, a few hours before the onset of the holiday that would have been his first without a pulpit.

There's nothing wrong with buying used things.

You know how much Israel means to me. And within Israel, the city of Jerusalem holds a special place in my heart. I believe as Danny Siegel did when he wrote that he'd rather smell the garbage in Jerusalem than the flowers anywhere else. I think the rabbis were right when they taught that Jerusalem is located directly under God's throne and so prayers spoken in Jerusalem ascend directly to God's Holy Place (perhaps that's why liturgy has always resonated more powerfully for me in Israel than anywhere else). All of which is to say that you should forge your own relationship with Israel. For you, Noam, it may be about hiking or dancing or spending time with family there. For you, Kayla, it may be about literature, the desert, the cultural life. There are many Israels and many ways to own her. Just make sure that the homeland of the Jewish people in some way becomes your own personal home too.

Noam, I know your observance of Shabbat has become less than meticulous lately. You will have to come to your own sense of what you want your religious observance to be. But I know for a fact how important it is to keep something of Shabbat in your life each week.

When you daven, try to experience the beauty of the liturgical language anew each time you say it. I know this can be hard, since we are repeating the same liturgy over and over, but it can help if you adopt some piece of the liturgy that is especially resonant for you. For me, this is the "Eelu Pheenu Maleh Shirah Ka'yam" section of the Nishmat prayer. The sheer poetry never fails to move me:

> *Were our mouths filled with song like the sea,*
> *were our tongues filled with rejoicing like the multitudes of*
> *    its waves,*
> *were our lips filled with praise as the wide-extended skies,*
> *were our eyes to shine with light like the sun and the moon,*

*were our hands to spread forth like the eagles of the sky,*
*were our feet as swift as the wild deer,*
*still we would be unable to thank You and bless Your name*
*for even one thousandth*
*or one ten-thousandth*
*of the myriad of bounty which You have bestowed upon*
   *our ancestors and upon us.*

Our davening is filled with themes and language that will resonate for you if you take the time to acquaint yourself with the language.

What Rabbi Leib Saras taught about Torah is important to think about for raising children too. He taught that a pious person is not one who preaches Torah; rather, a pious person is one who lives Torah. This is exactly true in raising children. We parents are all of us sometimes guilty of talking the talk without walking the walk. But we have to try, as best we can, to live our lives understanding that the only thing our children will understand about what we value and believe is what they see us *do* with our own lives. This is the reason that I made you come with me to services on Shabbat when you were still under my "jurisdiction" (i.e., during your preteenage years). I wanted you to hear the liturgy and absorb its cadences osmotically, even when you were so young that you were toddlers hanging out in the back of the room with the other kids. I wanted you to look up and see me davening and know that davening is important to me. And, most of all, I wanted you to learn that the reason I go to synagogue on Shabbat is that *I* need to be there, not because I think that since *you* should be there, I should be willing to immolate myself on the altar of sacrifice to make that happen.

When it comes time to raise children, do everything you can to raise them yourself (with your partner). Although I know some people have absolutely no choice, I am not, in general, a believer in letting others raise our children. One reason is that the gift of your real presence in their lives is truly, truly the *only* thing you have to give your children. But there is another reason. Many years ago, I got on a bus with both of you, Noam and Kayla. The bus was crowded, but I managed finally to maneuver all of us to seats near the back of the bus. Sometime later, a nanny got on the bus with a child who looked to be about six years old. The nanny waited at the front of the bus until she could snare a seat for the child, while she herself continued to stand. An elderly woman got onto the bus and, unable to find a seat, stood holding on to the overhead strap in front of the child's seat. I watched interestedly, curious to see if the nanny would urge the child to give up his seat to the elderly woman. The nanny made no move to do so, and as I thought about it later, I realized that to the nanny, her job was to make sure that that child was comfortable, safe, and happy. Happy, in this context, meant a seat. Only the parents could have taught that child the value of "respecting the elderly." And when the parents aren't available to teach, such teaching doesn't get done.

One of my rules is that we eat together as a family every night. This has become increasingly rare in America, and it was not always easy for us either, but I still think it is a good thing.

As a child, Kayla, you used to like to make apple-seed jewelry. We used to save the seeds from apples as we ate them, and we would let them dry out in a dish (if we didn't have enough apple seeds, we would hurriedly eat an apple or two and press anyone visiting us into service as an apple eater too). Then we used heavy thread and a big needle and sewed the seeds into rings and bracelets. You would adorn yourself with the jewelry on Shabbat and, in my eyes, you looked like the Shabbat Queen.

I know you both will remember our chocolate chip cookie gorges before Shabbat. I would multiply the chocolate chip cookie recipe by twenty and form the raw dough into twenty rolls, which I would freeze. Then before Shabbat each week, we would take a roll from the freezer, slice it still frozen, bake it, gorge ourselves on the first half dozen, and have fresh cookies for the rest of Shabbat. Good cookies. Good memories.

When on a trip with a child, take along Colorforms, which stick to the windows of planes and cars.

Ben and I wait with agonized impatience for those times when you both come home from college. After I've gotten my turn at hugging you both, one of my deepest private joys is to watch the three of you reconnect. You all huddle and snuggle together on the couch, Ben sandwiched between his two adored older siblings, laughing, poking, tickling, joking, hugging, until you've resoldered all the connections.

In my best-of-all-possible-worlds scenario, all three of you (I have to include ten-year-old Ben in this fantasy too) will grow up, get married, have many, many babies, and live in New York, near me, so I can adore your children as I have adored you. To encourage you in this, let me tell you that New York is one of the finest places in the world to raise kids. For one thing, I love living in a place where I know Ben and I will pass people speaking Spanish, Russian, Polish, Arabic, Korean, Hebrew, and English in the ten blocks it takes us to walk to the Heschel School. I don't like to live in a homogenized neighborhood and I never wanted to raise you kids anywhere else.

Never let an infant cry if you can help it. All you are teaching him is that, in this world, it is possible for a person's pain or discomfort to be ignored—which, after all, he will have to learn soon enough, but hopefully not from his parents.

Noam, you and I laughed until we howled the day you came home from high school and told me that your gay-rights-activist teacher had shown you a newspaper picture of two brides accompanied by a wedding announcement indicating that the couple had been married by a priest and a rabbi. "Bet this wedding announcement would make your mother crazy!" chortled the teacher. "You can bet on that!" you replied with strong conviction. "Most women hate lesbians," he commented. "Lesbians?" you replied in momentary confusion. "Who said anything about lesbians? My mother hates intermarriage!" Which, after I finished laughing, made me feel very content knowing that even as you make your own life decisions, I had succeeded in teaching you my bottom line. That's one of my strong life rules: Let your kids know your bottom line early and often in life. Mine was *no intermarriage*. I don't believe there's any point in being ambiguous about my bottom line, and I wanted to make sure that you knew that I meant business about this issue.

Buying undershirts for children is a waste of money. Buy short-sleeved shirts that they can wear in the summer and use as undershirts in the winter.

When you were a child, Kayla, you loved to lie in the sun, peer intently into flowers, and gaze raptly at bugs. I loved this quality in you.

Hang a red ribbon on the crib of a newborn. This will serve as protection from the evil eye. Nancy Trichter told me that when she brought Jacob home from the hospital, her mother was there, along with the baby nurse, to greet them at the door. As Nancy brought the baby into the house and moved to put Jacob into his new crib, her mother suddenly leaped into action, forestalling her by snatching Jacob out of her arms and thrusting him at the baby nurse. "Don't put him down in that crib yet; just hold him until I get back!" she called out frantically to the nurse as she rushed from the apartment. She reappeared ten minutes later, breathless, and attached a newly purchased red ribbon to the crib before the bemused eyes of the baby nurse, who merely remarked, "In Panama, we use blue."

Each day, ask your child to tell you three things that happened to him. You'll be surprised quite often by the things you will hear.

Try to coax your children into coming with you on errands instead of staying home (Noam!). Lots of important conversations in our family began in the frozen foods section of the supermarket.

You know that I never allowed any of you to have a TV or computer in your bedrooms. The last thing I wanted was for you children to be able to isolate yourselves away from the family for hours at a time.

When you become a parent, keep a TV and VCR in your bedroom and encourage your kids to watch TV there with you, sprawled on your bed or snuggled under your covers. You don't, however, have to let them eat tortilla chips (Noam!) while they're there.

More people know how to say no than know how to say yes. Try to say yes unless there's a reason to say no.

A month after my mother died, my father called me and announced, "Someone has to deal with the attic." My heart quailed as I hastily began to decline the honor, but my father forestalled me, stating firmly that he "didn't feel well enough" to handle it by himself (or at all, as it turned out). Resigned to my fate, I glumly promised to be there the following week. What greeted me when I arrived was virtually indescribable—an array, in glorious abandon, of eleven sets of dishes, all in their original packing cases; fourteen toasters; seven sets of pots and pans; eight sets of silverware; six clocks; five packing crates filled with stationery supplies; various trunks filled with linens; boxes of old toys and games, clocks, hot trays, popcorn poppers, electric can openers, model train sets, electric Crock-Pots, three generations' worth of clothes, not to mention four by now politically incorrect and therefore unwearable fur coats. My father, in the midst of beating a hasty retreat, turned around to announce virtuously that all of this accumulation was my mother's doing. "Right!" I called out bitterly to his receding back (and hairline). "Like you never participated in the family craziness of moving money every six months when the banks were giving away toasters for new accounts! And by the way," I pursued with increasing volume and frustration, "which bank was giving out that new color TV set of yours in the living room!" (Rhode Island Hospital Trust, as it turned out.) All of which taught me the validity of the rule I have always followed since then: If you own something you don't need, give it away to someone who can use it. Many people are afraid to do this, since they think there may come a time when they need the thing that they've given away. Believe me, it's better to give it away. Out of all the things you give away, there may be one you find you need. For that one thing, you'll figure out a way to replace it. And in the meantime, someone will have been able to use and derive pleasure from all the other stuff you really didn't need.

I always believed in taking you kids out of school every now and then for a few days or a week to go on a family vacation or to visit relatives. I reasoned that you were likely to learn some mighty important life lessons from hanging out with the family, and these lessons would serve you in at least as good stead as algebra was likely to.

Also, I allowed each of you to stay home from school every now and then when you felt you needed a break. Noam, you used to be especially shameless about this—looking theatrically wan and announcing that you felt a fever coming on and thought you should stay home in case it arrived when you were in school. As soon as I would ask you if you felt you needed a day off, you would sigh in contentment and reply, "Yup!" We'd often have wonderful days, building elaborate Lego structures, or curled up in bed watching old movies, or shopping for books at Barnes and Noble.

Try to cook with your children as often as possible. It slows you down, as an adult, which is a good thing; it helps your children learn the art of cooking, which every person needs to know; and you get the added bonus of hanging out together.

As a toddler, Ben used to routinely throw temper tantrums in the street. I don't even remember anymore what triggered the tantrums. I do remember that he could not tolerate being touched or spoken to during these episodes. I developed the technique of standing nearby, not making eye contact with him, letting him scream until he was able to begin to calm himself. My own nerves in shreds, I would quietly suggest after a while that we move on, which, more often than not, he was ready to do. I can't tell you how many times people came up to me to comment harshly on his behavior or mine. It often took all my strength not to respond, but what I wanted to say to them was "Can you not spare some pity for the parent who is not abusive but is at her wit's end?"

On the other hand, if you think you are in danger of killing your child, let him cry and you walk away. I learned this when Noam was two years old. Aunt Betty, who had come for a visit from Memphis, was temporarily living with us because Uncle Davey had developed a leg infection and had been admitted to a hospital near our house. She was on the telephone with one of Uncle Davey's doctors, who was trying to prepare her for the possibility of a leg amputation, while I stood nearby offering moral support. Just then, I heard a knock at the door. I answered to find both our downstairs neighbors in the hallway asking in alarm what was going on in our house, explaining that the ceilings in both their bathrooms had suddenly collapsed and water was pouring down from our floor. I raced to the bathroom, wrenched open the door, and was greeted by a flood of surging water. I waded my way upstream into the bathroom and found two-year-old Noam perched on the washing machine staring apprehensively at me, having managed to turn on all the water faucets because he wanted to see if the room could fill up with water (it could and did). On the heels of Uncle Davey's medical crisis, I knew I had reached my limit. I picked Noam up in my arms and silently marched upstairs with him to his room. He was clearly terrified by my silence and did not utter a sound. I deposited him in his crib and left the room, quietly closing the door behind me. Noam waited a full minute and then tentatively began to wail. I made a move to open the door to his room, and then, looking down at my hand on the door handle, I realized I was shaking. I also realized that this was the moment when, if I were prone to physical violence, I would have hit my son. Instead, I walked downstairs, apologized to my neighbors, and reassured them that I would pay for the installation of new ceilings in their apartments, as well as for any other water damage. They left; I made the calls to the carpenter and plasterer; and then, having organized the repairs, I went into my bedroom, closed the door, and began to weep.

Try to have people over for dinner frequently. Try, as well, to invite out-of-town family and friends to visit. Your lives can only be enriched by letting the private space of family expand to embrace the presence of others. Our Shabbat table frequently rivaled that of our friends Art and Kathy Green—and they were well known for effortlessly hosting twenty-five friends and neighbors for dinner.

I believe in creating new family traditions that serve the needs of our family as those needs change. Once Kayla became a vegetarian, the notion of the traditional Thanksgiving dinner became, for our family, obsolete. That's when we started the tradition of each person choosing one favorite food. All the foods formed a menu that we all cooked together on Thanksgiving Day.

Cousin Lenny died very unexpectedly recently. Everyone in the family loved Lenny, and as word of his sudden death circulated, everyone in the family cleared their calendars to be able to attend the funeral. That's when I realized that anyone, on twenty-four hours' notice, will make time to go to the funeral of someone they care about. Not everyone, however, sets aside the time to go to weddings, Bar or Bat Mitzvahs, and baby celebrations. This is wrong. I learned this from Cousin Estelle, who has a personal policy of, wherever possible, attending every family *simcha*. I once asked her why she was flying to Israel for the wedding of a distant cousin. Surprised by the question, she replied, "Because they invited me and they are family."

The greatest gift in my life has been my children. Many parents feel this way, but it is not something we talk about easily.

Since the day you were born, I have added the following prayer when I *bench licht* (light candles) on Friday nights. "Dear God, please let my children grow to be mentally, emotionally, and physically healthy."

Raising teenage children can sometimes be so excruciatingly painful that parents are not sure that their hearts will not be broken irreparably in the process. That is what happened to my friend Felice. She was a religious Jewish single parent whose twenty-one-year-old daughter began to seriously date a non-Jew. The situation between her and Jenny, her daughter, rapidly deteriorated to such an extent that the two, who had been so close, literally were not able to speak to or even look at each other. Felice's heart was broken and, in desperation, she sought advice from a therapist on how to handle the situation without losing her daughter or having to accept something that was antithetical to everything she believed. The therapist helped her unravel some of the emotional skeins. After a month of meetings, the therapist opened a session by asking: "Is there something that belongs to you that your daughter really loves—some piece of jewelry or a family heirloom or an article of clothing perhaps?" "Certainly," replied Felice, "but so what? I can't give her a present now when we are quite literally not speaking. She's not stupid. She would see right through that!" "Don't be so sure of what it is that your daughter will see," responded the therapist. "Just as strongly as you are missing your daughter, is she probably missing her mother. We just need a way for you to tell her and for her to understand that even though she has tripped over your bottom line, you want her to know that she will always have your unequivocal love." "I'm willing to try this if you help me rehearse how to do it," replied Felice, "but I'm frankly skeptical about my ability to offer the gift in the right way without her throwing it back in my face!" Two weeks later, Felice worked on summoning her courage, having practiced what she wanted to say. As Jenny entered the house, Felice's throat closed up in terror at what was at stake and she had to force the words through a solid barrier. It took every ounce of her courage and all of her determination to reconnect with her daughter when Felice, for the first time in months, looked directly into her daughter's face and said, "Jenny, I want you to have my mother's pin—the one you've always loved." "Me?" replied Jenny in amazement. "Why would you give it to me?" "Because," answered Felice, trying desperately hard to say it right, "You're the one I fell in love with twenty-one years ago. You're the one who will always be my daughter. And you're the one who is heir to my mother's and your mother's pins and hopes and love."

Noam, you've pretty much stopped learning any Jewish text for now. Try to stay open to the possibility of coming back to study when you are ready. Keep in mind that Rabbi Akiva only began to learn the Hebrew alphabet at the age of forty, but thirteen years later, he was a teacher of Torah and was regarded as a light of his generation.

Your father once went to a party shortly after Noam was born. With a newborn and a two-year-old, I was too depressed and exhausted even to contemplate such an outing. The notion of finding a babysitter, of expressing enough breast milk before the event to last Noam for a few hours, and of showering and finding something other than a bathrobe to wear seemed about as feasible to me as climbing the Himalayas. So your father went and bumped into Bob, whom he hadn't seen in ten years. They caught up on their lives and then, noticing Bob's wife's absence, your father asked where Shoshana was. "Oh, she's home crying in the bathroom," replied Bob. "That's amazing!" replied your father. "That's exactly where Sharon is too!" The memory of the exhaustion and desperation I felt in those days is still so real to me almost twenty years later that I sometimes volunteer my services as a babysitter to the parents of newborns for an afternoon or evening.

I've never believed in letting you children get too territorial, just as I myself am not too territorial. When we've had guests stay over, I've expected you to switch rooms or double up with siblings. I've never asked your permission, you kids have never demurred, and today you are all extremely flexible about your personal environments—which is, I think, a good thing.

Most women I know who have a career as well as a family live lives comprised in equal measures of patched-together organization and quiet desperation.

In late-twentieth-century America, humility is unfashionable. We do not teach our children to remain humble, we teach them to become strong. These two are not exactly incompatible, but they don't necessarily sit easily together. And while I value strength and aggressiveness about as much as anyone, I've always thought it is also important to teach you children to remain humble. Otherwise we risk losing sight of just where it is all this strength comes from.

You cannot conceive yet how deeply it is possible to love your children, but I pray that one day you will understand this.

The way to love your children is to give them the tools they will need to function as responsible adults in the world. Paradoxically, this requires you, as parents, to do the one thing you don't ever want to do—let your children grow away from you.

I admire my friend Maggie, who is an obstetrician. At first, when one of her children began to have problems in school, she hired tutors and specialists. When the problems only continued to grow, she decided that what her daughter needed was for her to set aside the time to address seriously what was going on with her. So she took a leave of absence from her work for more than a year, until she felt that her daughter's problems had been handled.

Don't ever have surgery that requires anesthesia unless you absolutely have to. Doctors tend to give us statistics about the risks of anesthesia and the statistical risk always seems so small that we ignore it. My friend's mother, however, had a toe operation and died of the anesthesia.

I think the large-size IKEA bags are the strongest bags around.

Always hide a twenty-dollar bill in your wallet for emergencies. And don't use it for anything other than emergencies (Noam!).

Always carry food and water when you are out with a child.

On a long flight, take off your shoes, drink lots of water (take bottled water with you), and walk around as much as you can.

Know how to be warm and friendly, but don't let people walk all over you. This is an important truth for both of you.

All my life, when someone whose judgment I respected would casually tell me they'd found "the best" math tutor or dance instructor or tax attorney, I would jot down the information in my Rolodex (along with the recommender's name) in case I ever needed the information later. When you're in a crisis, trying to locate the best body shop will feel a lot less daunting if you already have the information in your Rolodex under "B."

As soon as practical after you get a spot on a piece of clothing, get some soap and water and wash it out. If you have nothing else, a little shampoo or dishwashing detergent will do.

Once, a dry cleaner refused to take responsibility for dry cleaning my very expensive jacket. My friend Helayne Gordon, who always offers unfailingly good advice, advised me to throw it into the washing machine. I did, the jacket was fine, and I learned to keep my brain engaged when reading manufacturers' warning labels.

On the same subject, you *can* remove the manufacturer's tags from mattresses without fear of government reprisal.

Carry your wallet in your front pocket to avoid pickpockets. Noam, this means you. Remember what a pain it was for you to replace everything when your wallet was pickpocketed while you were on the number 1 train last year?

You don't have to peel potatoes to make latkes or kugels. Just wash the skins really well.

Never work on someone's behalf who is not willing to work on his own behalf.

I was once casually acquainted with a man named Tom, who was arrested on a serious felony charge. He called to tell me what had happened and to ask for my financial help in hiring a lawyer to defend him. As we spoke, I thought about how sad is was that Tom had turned to me for help at this moment of crisis in his life instead of his family. I asked him about his family. He replied that his mother was dead, that his father had abandoned the family at the time of his parents' divorce, and that he had not seen his father in the ensuing forty years. I told him that I would think about his request overnight and would give him an answer the next day. I did think about it a lot that night, weighing my beliefs against his need. The next day I called him and made the following offer: I would give him the money he needed if he called his father to solicit financial help from him first. Tom was aghast at my proposal and absolutely refused to consider it. His distress caused me grave misgivings, but I did not back down, because I have a deeply held belief that "family takes care of family." Before I am willing to help someone who is not my family, I want to know that the person has turned first to those who should be the ones to offer support. I told Tom that my offer would stay open forever, and that he could come back to me at any time if he changed his mind. Two weeks later, I got a call from him. He had been thinking about my proposal and he was willing to try it. During our conversation, he asked me twice whether his father had to actually give him money or whether he himself merely had to ask for it, and when I reassured him for the second time, I finally understood how terribly traumatizing this phone call would be for him. I nearly wavered, but then my instincts reasserted themselves and I merely wished him luck. Two days later, Tom called back. He told me that his father had burst into tears when Tom told him who he was. His father explained that he had tried to see Tom after the divorce, but that Tom's mother had prevented it. For forty years, he had hoped to meet up with his son again, and now the phone call had opened that door. Tom's father was himself struggling financially, but when he heard about Tom's problem, he immediately offered to take a loan against his insurance policy. As Tom told me with deep excitement about their conversation and about the appointment they had made to meet, I found myself feeling astonished and slightly sickened by my own hubris in insisting on superimposing my values on a situation that, but for God's generosity, could have ended painfully for Tom instead of happily.

Don't blame others when you screw up. Accept responsibility for your own actions (I've heard enough self-justification to last me a lifetime!). Try all your life to see clearly what your own role has been in any situation.

When you cook fish, you need to be quite exact on the time. I think it's best to turn off the oven before it's completely done.

The residual heat will finish the cooking process and by the time you take it to the table, it will be perfect.

This may sound harsh, but don't keep up relationships if you don't want to. Figure out how to end the relationship and then don't back down if someone cries or whines at you. Kayla, even though you are the more "sensitive" one in the family, you've always been able to exercise a kind of steely resolve when you've wanted to end a relationship. It's Noam I worry about. You, Noam, sometimes take more abuse than you should in some of your relationships, believing somehow that if you want to be a real friend, you will have to tolerate just about anything (I'm thinking about the friend who used our house for a rendezvous with his girlfriend without letting you know about it, leaving you exposed to my wrath).

You don't have to throw out leftover salad if you've dressed it. To save a salad dressed with an oil dressing for the next day, take a small plate and put it upside down at the bottom of a large bowl. Put the salad on top of the plate and the dressing will drip down and leave the salad crisp for the next day.

If you wear glasses, always take a spare pair when you travel.

When you have your car repaired, staple a note to the generally illegible bill, indicating the date and nature of the repair. Save the bills in chronological order in your car. That way, when your tire goes flat, as mine did last year, within the guarantee period, you will actually have the paper you need with you when you need to prove the date of purchase.

I know it sounds like a cliché, but we are big believers in the helpfulness of good therapists when you need them (the operative word here is *good*—there are lots of lousy therapists around; you need to find someone with wisdom and insight). I know you, Noam, are moaning right about now. But you have to admit that there were times when your load was immeasurably lightened by the presence of someone who could listen neutrally to you complain about me!

One of the difficult judgments all parents have to make is when and how to offer help to their children. No parent wants to see his child suffer, but we all know that it is easy to ruin a person by not letting him grow into himself. And real growth only happens through travail.

# Basic Life Rules

Take care of your body. This is very important. If something seems wrong with you, *never put off investigating it*. And treat your body with the reverence and care God did in blessing you with it.

Take care of yourself and your family first. This is not an easy one for me. Creating the right priorities is something I've struggled with all my life, so I know how important it is.

Making love is not the same thing as eating pizza. They may both involve basic human instincts, but sex involves responsibility to the other. Never be intimate with someone you don't care about.

About something else I am absolutely certain. There definitely is a God who has a plan for the world.

I've told you this since you were young; it's my most serious life rule: *Carpe diem.*

Secrets in a family are bad. The repercussions can reverberate for generations. When you are ready to hear them, I will tell you all the secrets you need to know.

*Never* let your work, no matter how engrossing or important it may be to you, interfere with your family. *Never. Never. Never.* This is one of the most important basic life rules.

You must always be proactive in terms of your own or a loved one's medical care. Never let a doctor make decisions that are, by rights, yours to make. Be vigilant.

Don't waste. Whether it be time, resources, or money, waste is a sin.

When you find yourself in an unhealthy place, leave immediately. You can get sucked into an unhealthy environment faster than you would believe.

The corollary to the point above is that there are some people who are toxic. When you find yourself around destructive people, get away from them. Toxic people pollute their immediate environment.

Never let anyone else manage your money. Don't let other people invest your money for you. Don't take stock tips from anyone, no matter how brilliant they are in business.

I have invariably lost money when I have given over decision making or control to anyone else—and this includes relatives and friends. No one will ever pay as much attention to your money as you (unless you are a fool).

Never believe a doctor who tells you there is no hope. Life and death, I am absolutely certain, rest in God's hands alone.

Always keep in mind where you come from.

Trust your instincts in life. Always believe that your instinct is right, and don't let others try to convince you that your instinct is not your instinct.

Accept who you are. Don't be at war with yourself.

Always protect your siblings. They are your best friends and will always look out for you, as you must look out for them.

I'VE ALWAYS been fascinated by Moses, who is, for me, one of the most interesting, most complicated, and in many ways, most tragic figures in our history. If we study the commentaries, we learn that there are many different Moseses, but the Moses I know best is the Moses as parent. This Moses is charged with helping the Children of Israel grow from infancy into adolescence on their forty-year journey. He devotes his life to the task of leading this people on their grand quest for the Promised Land—which is, at some symbolic level, the place where Moses knew his adolescent People of Israel could emerge, finally, as fully formed adults. And in a final irony, as Moses himself stood on Mount Nebo, where he could look across the plains and see that Promised Land and know his work was coming to fruition, God intervened to tell him that he would not be the one to lead them into that land. Moses' own personal journey had ended outside the boundaries of the Promised Land. And in that irony, God taught all of us parents an important lesson. We do the best we can while we have our children at our sides. Finally, though, our job is to let them go to find their own promised lands—to places we too will never be allowed to enter.

# Postscript to My Children

*I'm done raising you; you'll be starting your own journey now. I have tremendous faith in your intelligence, clarity, and honesty. And I pray that what you choose to take with you on your journey will provide you with all the sustenance and nurturing you will need along the way. With all my heart, I love you and wish you* tzet-cha le-shalom *("may you go toward peace").*

*Love,*

*eema*

SHARON STRASSFELD is a well-known author and activist both in- and outside the Jewish community. Her works include *The Jewish Calendar*, *The Jewish Family Book*, and three editions of *The Jewish Catalog*. Ms. Strassfeld is a builder and owns a café and real estate business. She lives in Manhattan and is the mother of three.